QuickBooks Online 2024
For Beginners

I0427240

The Definitive Quick Learning Manual for QBO, packed with Practical Examples and Detailed Explanations

DEMAC VINZ

© Copyrights 2023 – all rights reserved.

The contents of this book may not be reproduced, duplicated, or transmitted without direct written permission from the author or publisher.

No blame or legal responsibility will be held against the publisher or author for any damages, reparations, or monetary loss due to the information contained in this book. Whether directly or indirectly.

Disclaimer notice:

Please note that the information within this document is for educational and entertainment purposes only. All efforts have been made to present reliable and complete information; no warranties are implied or declared.

The trademarks used are without any consent, and the publication of the trademark is without permission or backing by the owner. All trademarks and brands within this book are for clarifying purposes only and are owned by the owners, not affiliated with this document

Table Of Content

Introduction

One of the challenges small business faces is financial management which is often complex. This challenge is addressed with the correct resources, applications and information. QuickBooks Online is the most popular cloud accounting software and an effective tool which permits small business and companies to optimize financial procedure that guarantees accuracy, conserves energy and save valuable work time.

It is designed for small businesses and companies by an American company called Intuit. The company also make TurboTax, Mint and MailChimp. It is a safe place where you can record and store all of your business's transactions. QuickBooks Online makes it super simple to check your profit and cash flow which is key for any small business. This guide will lead you step by step through every feature of this interesting program hence giving you the understanding and ability to utilize its full potentials.

You have the chance in this book to learn everything there is to know about this program and why small and large businesses around the world rely on it.

Though QuickBooks has its desktop version but what we are talking about here is the online version. The online version has an advantage and that is that you will be able to access your company file from anywhere you happen to be that has internet access. If you work out in the field for example, you might have your laptop with you or need to access it through your phone and these are great reasons to sign up with a subscription for the QuickBooks online service.

We are going to be taking this from the very beginning. I'm not going to assume you know anything. I'm going to actually start off showing you how to go online and pick the correct subscription. We will talk a little bit about working with QuickBooks Online and mobile devices and then we will take it from there and start actually setting up our company file. As you read through this book, you will learn how to deal with; Receivable accounts. Payroll

How to create invoices: what to do when a customer pays you and how to actually put that money in the bank.

We will also discuss the other side, which is your accounts payable, or anything related to the mail you receive and the invoices you have to pay. To ensure that you always know how much you owe, you should keep track of those. We will be going over and discussing a little bit about goods and services (which are tangible items and occasionally your services that you offer), but occasionally you purchase goods and you sell goods as well, so we need to know how to set this up correctly.

We wish to assist you in selecting the QuickBooks Online edition that best meets your requirements, so we will have examined and explained each of its variations.

You will be equipped with the knowledge to manage your finances independently after this experience.

This book explains how QuickBooks online may improve your company's financial management and empower you to make informed decisions that will help your business grow and succeed. So, let's explore this incredible software's possibilities together as we walk through it

Chapter One

What Is This QuickBooks Online

QuickBooks online is cutting – edge cloud-based accounting software created by Intuit to streamline and simplify several facets of financial management for companies, independent contractors, and other self – employed people. it is a flexible solution for enterprise of all sizes since it provides various tools and capabilities that cater to different financial demands.

The primary function is to operate as a central digital hub for managing financial transactions, keeping track of spending, creating invoices and keeps records on cash flows. QuickBooks online unlike other conventional desktop accounting software function in the cloud which enable users to view their financial information and detail anywhere they are from any device with internet access. All data on QuickBooks online are safely kept and backed up because of the cloud's nature, improving accessibility and lowering loss of data likelihood.

With its cloud-based platform, QuickBooks online has become a game changing force in the world of accounting software, revolutionizing how companies of all sizes handle their financial operation. QuickBooks online offers a full range of solutions to expedite and simplify various facets of financial administration, each specifically tailored to fit the need of small to medium-sized business, freelancers, and independent contractors.

QuickBooks online was designed from ground up to be simple to use and intuitive. As a result, task previously tricky and time consuming, such as bookkeeping, creating financial reports, and keeping track of cost, may now be completed quickly and effectively. Since the software's user interface is intended to be usable by people with different degrees of financial competence, it can be valuable for business owners who may not have strong accounting backgrounds.

Real-time collaboration facilitation is one of QuickBooks online's outstanding features. This is especially important for companies that uses remote workers, scattered teams, or outsourced accountants.

Multiple people may access and edit financial data simultaneously, facilitating more efficient workflows, precise data entry, and transparency in financial procedures.

Additionally, QuickBooks online is aware of the various requirements of businesses and the equipment they use. It readily connects with a broad range of third-party application, from systems for processing payments to those for e-commerce, enabling customers to customize the program to meet their unique company needs.

This integration option highlights the flexibility and adaptability of QuickBooks online, giving it a solution that can develop along with an expanding organization.

QuickBooks online provides a complete solution, whether you are a small company owner trying to manage your finance better, a freelancer trying to keep track of revenue and spending, or an accountant working the books for several customers.

Its cloud-based makes data to be secure, safely kept and made available from anywhere, allowing company owners and professionals to access their financial data while on transit.

The software has completely changed the accounting software environment by offering a user friendly, collaborative, and customizable platform. With a wide range of capabilities, it enables businesses to take charge of their financial management, promoting informed choice and nurturing the overall success and expansion of the organization it supports.

QuickBooks online architecture encompasses:

1. Dashboard and overview: Users are welcomed with an easy-to-use dashboard that gives them a quick overview of their financial situation after checking in. This summary includes critical indicators, including income, costs, earnings and unpaid bills.

2. Invoicing: QuickBooks online streamlines the invoicing procedure by enabling users to create and modify attractive invoices. It facilitates cash flow management by tracking when bills are received, examined, and paid.

3. Expense Tracking: By typing bank accounts, credit cards, and other financial institutions to QuickBooks online, users can quickly record and classify company spending. The effort associated with human data entry is decreased by the software's automated import and categorization of transactions.

4. Automated bank reconciliation is a feature of QuickBooks online that compares imported transactions to those entered into the program. Accurate financial records are ensured, and mistakes are reduced as a result.

5. Reporting and analytics: The program creates several financial reports including cash flow statements, balance sheets, and profit and loss statements. Decision – making is aided by these reports' insights on the company's economic performance.

6. Payroll Management: Businesses may compute and handle employee salaries, taxes and deductions using QuickBooks online's integrated payroll services. This function contributes to prompt and accurate payroll processing.

7. Integration: Various third-party software and solution, including payment processors, e-commerce platforms, and CRM systems, are easily integrated with QuickBooks online. This integration improves the usefulness and flexibility of the program to different business demands.

8. Multi-User collaboration: organization may work together in real -time within QuickBooks online with several team members or outside accountants. This function promotes practical cooperation and guarantees the most recent financial information access.

9. Mobile accessibility: Users may manage their money on the move by taking receipt photos, sending bills, and seeing financial reports from their smartphones or tables using a dedicated mobile app.

QuickBooks online is a sophisticated cloud-based accounting tool that enables businesses to manage their finance effectively, analyze transactions, produce reports, and make financially sound choices. It is an indispensable and gain more financial management due to its user-friendly design, real-time collaboration features, and interaction with external technologies.

Benefits of using QuickBooks Online for small businesses

For small companies, using QuickBooks online has many advantages, altering how they handle their money and promoting overall expansion and success. Here are a few significant benefits:

1. Accessibility and convenience: Because QuickBooks Online is cloud-cloud, users may access financial data from any location anytime if they have an internet connection. Even on the go, decision-making may be done quickly because of this accessibility.

2. Time savings: QuickBooks online' automation capabilities significantly decrease the need for human data entry. Automatic import and categorization of bank transaction can save time that could be better used for necessary company operations.

3. Simplified Invoicing: it is now simple to create and send expert invoices. Faster cash flow is made possible by QuickBooks Online' customized templates,

automated payment reminders, and the ability to monitor when invoices are opened and paid.

4. Accurate Financial Tracking: Business owners may precisely monitor their financial health with real-time tracking of revenue and spending making.

5. Financial Reporting: several built-in reports, including profit and loss statements, balance sheets, and cash flow statements, are available in QuickBooks Online. Strategic planning is aided by these reports' insights into the company's financial performance.

QuickBooks Online Subscriptions

Registering for one of QuickBooks' subscription services is the first step you must take before utilizing the software. QuickBooks Online is not free to use; a monthly fee is required. There are four different membership options available. All you have to do is go to QuickBooks.Intuit.com, their website. You will see a variety of information on their membership services after logging on.

One thing I should mention is that you can test each one out for free for thirty days, so you can decide which one best suit your needs as a business and see whether you enjoy it before committing to a purchase. There are four versions/subscriptions of QuickBooks online available:

A. Simple Start

B. Essentials

C. Plus

D. Advanced.

If you have already decided which one to try, you may join up using the discount at $30 per month, or you can choose one and try it out for free during the 30-day trial. Depending on when you visit their website, the prices that you see could vary. Here's an example of what their website looks like when you log in:

As you can see from the above photo, there is a monthly price for each of these depending on when you visit the website. However, if you join up for three months at a once, you may currently receive 50% off. If you are a new firm with few clients or not much going on with your enterprise yet, you should start with the simple start. It is the most fundamental one. Starting with the basic version is a terrific idea, and you can easily upgrade when you require additional features. You can see the features of each membership you might want to join up for by scrolling down. You can only have one user for the basic start, which essentially implies that only one person will be able to log in using that username and password. If you require more, you can see that the essentials allow for up to three people, the plus allows for up to five, and the advanced allows for up to 25 users.

To take a closer look at every feature for each, let us scroll down for a moment:

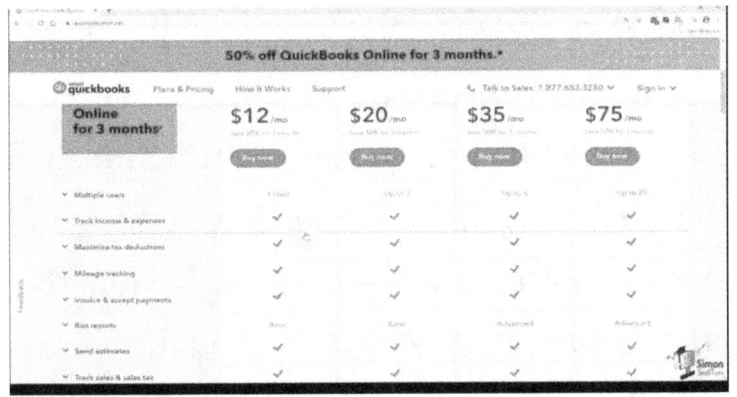

Other wonderful advantages of the Simple Start include the ability to track your upcoming expenses. All four of them let you accomplish that; they'll all help you get the most out of your tax deductions; they'll all have mileage, invoice, and take payments. They'll all have reports, too, but you'll notice that the basic start and the essential one to its right only provide the most basic reports; if you require more sophisticated reporting, you should choose the plus and advanced options. You will have a ton of reports, even with the basic ones. Reporting is one of QuickBooks' strongest points; estimations can be entered into all of these. One really wonderful thing that all construction companies have in common is that you would want to estimate a job before you actually start working on it and getting paid for it. As you scroll down, you'll see that all of these allow you to save and organize your receipts, so you can scan them in. You can also track sales and sales tax. All of these allow you to manage 1099 contractors, which is crucial because they are your subcontractors and you need to know how to treat them correctly. Whether you choose the basic, plus, or advanced plan, you will be able to handle the costs. You cannot handle the bills in QuickBooks with the basic start, which is incredibly crucial in my opinion because you need to keep track of everything you owe because you will need to strictly adhere to your budget when you initially launch your firm. I mentioned earlier that simple start is ideal for a small firm starting out because you can simply upgrade, but it also prevents you from measuring time or doing what they term tracking job profitability. The inventory feature is one that sometimes people want, and you would have to upgrade to the plus or advanced to get it. For the essentials, it simply lacks the job tracking profitability, the ability to send batch invoices, and really, if you don't do a lot of these things, they might not be important to you.

The most common subscription, the Plus, lacks the ability to import and send batch invoices as well as business analytics and insights options. However, you may not require these features, so if you do want all of that, you can upgrade to the advanced subscription.

Just relax about all of these; you already know that you might switch between these subscriptions because you might need to add users in order to have four or more people accessing QuickBooks. There are a number of factors to consider, and if you are unsure which would be ideal for your company, you can always give them a call. I wanted you to know that because the next step is to really begin with one of these. You have the option to either buy it right away or go to the top of the page to give it a try for free for 30 days

QuickBooks Online And Mobile Devices

Here will shall be discussing on how this amazing app works with mobile devices.

The first thing I want you to know is that your online version of QuickBooks is constantly evolving. You might log in one time and be used to where a particular option happens to be and the next time you log in it may not be there at all or may be in a different location or look different. Your friend might have a version and not see the updates that you see, but you will receive them eventually because they do not apply the changes to everyone simultaneously when they rule them out.

Additionally, depending on whether you have an iPhone or an Android smartphone, you can use separate mobile apps for QuickBooks that sync with the software. Look for the QuickBooks apps in the Play Store or the iPhone app store, and you can download them to carry with you wherever you go. For instance, if you need to create an invoice while out in the field, you can do it directly on your phone, and it will sync with your online version. Now, the apps will not have all of the options that are available but they will have the basic most common ones that you would want to use. go ahead also and look in your app store and see if there are other software apps that are not made by intuit but would work well with QuickBooks and it might be something that you might need in your business. There are all kind of apps that work with QuickBooks that want to make you aware of.

If you ever wanted to just get a handle on what some of the changes that they are making in your version, you can actually log into QuickBooks. Intuit. Comm /blog and then you will be able to see all of the changes and stay on top of what is new.

Chapter two

QuickBooks Online Sample/Company Files

In QuickBooks, a file you set up is referred to as a company. You are able to own as many businesses as you like. A small business owner may frequently create two companies: one with his personal information and the other with business information. You can have as many company files as you like, they don't communicate with one another, and you don't have to worry about data becoming mixed up.

In QuickBooks you have to either create a brand new one, you might already have the desktop version of QuickBooks and you want to upload your file to the online version which we will touch as we progress. However, even if you do not have a sample file, you can go in and play with as much as you want. You do not have to sign up with a subscription or anything like that to access the sample file. All you have to do is head on over to http://qbo.intuit.com/redir/testdrive and the company file you are going to be working with here is "Craig's design and landscaping services". It is a service-based business.

So, log on to the above and let us discuss the interface of Craig's design & landscaping services. The first thing you will have to do is just verify your real person. You are going to check the box "I'm not a robot" and then in this case it asked me to pick all the cars, you go through the list and make sure you got them all and hit verify.

Now it knows you are a real person and you can access Craig's design and landscaping services.

Before we continue, let me just mention a couple of other things about the sample file. Every day they update the date so, you will see that date change, you are actually going to be working in the year 2023 in the practice exercise. So, just kind of know that when you go in there and this is what QuickBooks looks like when you first open it up as you can see below;

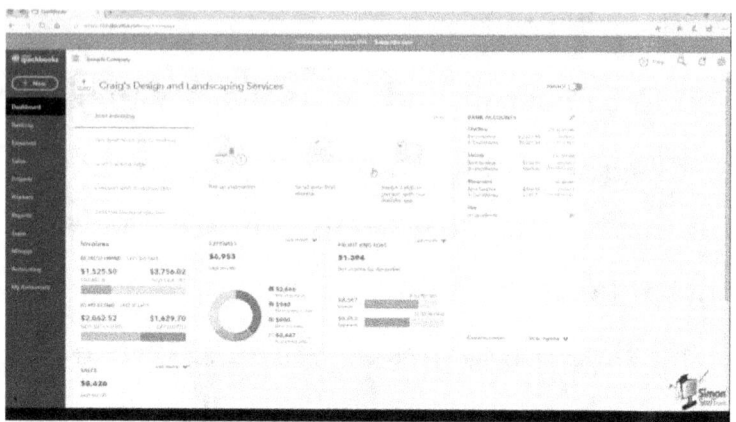

How To Create A New QuickBooks Online Account

Here we will be talking about how do you actually go through and set up your new QuickBooks online account. All we are going to do is navigate to where we looked at the different online subscriptions earlier and then we will go ahead and decide which of those subscriptions we would like to sign up with or we can sign up with a 30-day free trial.

let me go ahead and sign for that 30-day free trial and to show you how this works as you can navigated back to "quickbooks.intuit.com"

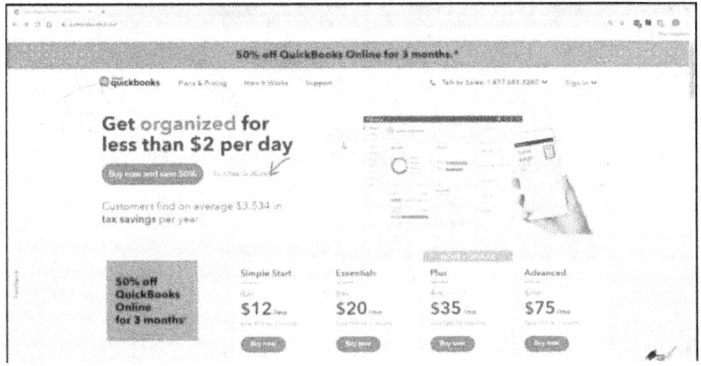

As we have decided to take advantage of the free 30-day trial, we are going to use the link as indicate with red arrow on the above picture. Right there, you see a pop-up that asks you if you would like to sign up with the 30-day free trial. You can use that option as well. What we are going to do here is to create an intuit account and we can do this a couple of different ways. Once you click on that link, it will take you to this prompt below;

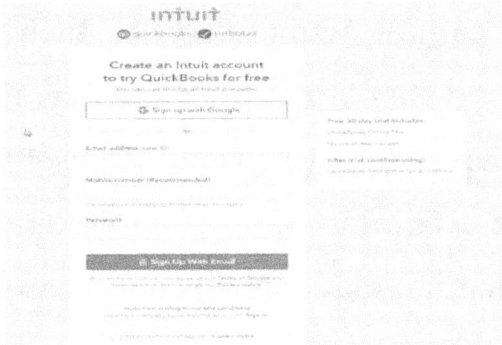

This shows that we can actually sign up in multiple ways be it with google, and if you have multiple Intuit products then, you can go ahead and use that one login for all of them. We might also choose to use an email address and sign up that way and for the purpose of this illustration, we will be signing in with email. So, you just input your mail address of your choice that is active and that you have access to. Also, it asks you to plug in your mobile number that is recommended but you may choose to ignore it though the reason that you may want to go ahead and do that is; if you happen to forget your username or your login information and - it can help you recover that information by looking at your telephone number that you have plugged in. Next, you will create a password and make sure it is something that you are going to remember but hard enough that someone else cannot actually try to get into account. Note that, a good password anywhere in your computer will have at least eight to twelve characters, you are going to have a combination of capital letters, small letters and you might have special characters. Once you are done with that, click sign up with email. What is going to happen now is, it is going to start setting up what we call our company file. Each file in QuickBooks is called a company, you can have as many companies as you like in QuickBooks. This is going to launch us through what is called the easy step interface where it is going to ask us some questions and based on how we answer those questions, it will set up all the options in our company file for us.

First, we will see some basic information, it wants to know what is the name of your business (you can type any business name of your choice for example, ABC) and then the next thing it will ask us is to describe the type of business we do. If you start typing in things like plumbing, electrical and things like that, then it is going to start pulling from a drop-down list and looking for those first few characters there and if you see something close to what you do on the list just choose it. There is no wrong answer here just choose something close to what you do and click Next. The next thing it will ask you is what would you like to do in QuickBooks and you might want to do a lot of these different things, you might want to send and attract invoices, organize your expenses, manage your inventory, track your sales (if you have retail sales you will want to choose it but if you don't, you may want to leave that), track your bills, track your sales tax ,pay your employees, and track your hours.

So, you can see that you can choose a few of these or all of these. Then click Next to the bottom and now it says what is your role at the business? are you an owner? are you the bookkeeper? The employee usually the owner of the company is the one that sets up the file or it could have been that the accountant set it up for the owner, whichever person sets it up is actually going to be the admin or the administrator of the file; meaning that you will actually own it. So, you can choose accordingly. If I scroll down a little bit, you will see that it says "do you have an accountant or bookkeeper right now" and you do not have to say yes even if you do have one. It is just asking you this because it is going to set up some of the options as we go down the road for the accountant.

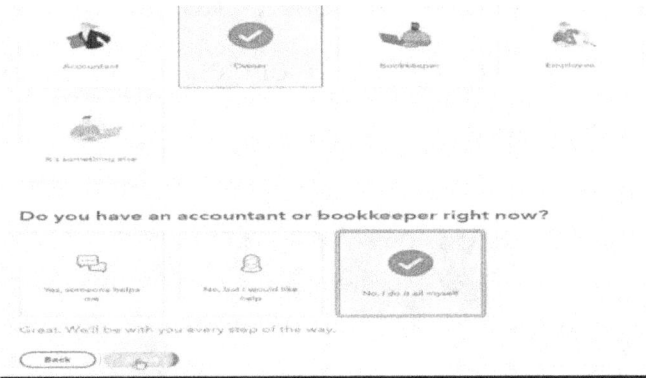

So, I clicked the "no, do it all by myself" and click all set button. Now what you have is a basic setup for your QuickBooks company file.

There are still a lot we have to do because, it is really a blank company file right now but at least we have the file set up so that we can work on it. If you wanted to go through a 30 second tour to help you get down to business on QuickBooks, you can do that.

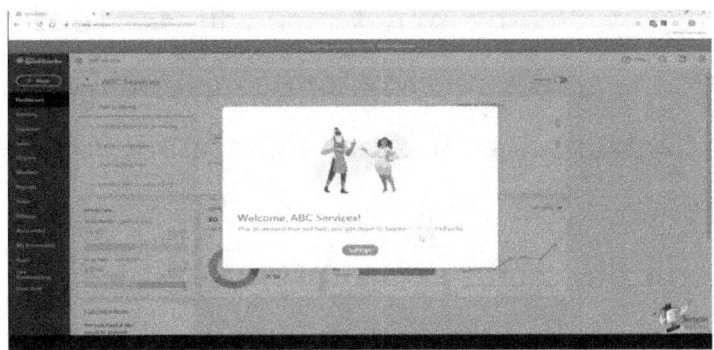

You can now go ahead and close that out and then, below is what it looks like when you first log in, you are on what is called the dashboard and the dashboard is just a quick way to see an overview of how different areas of your company.

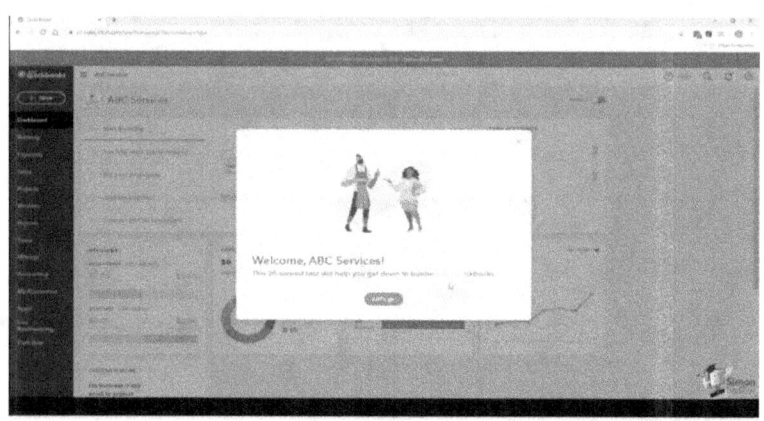

We refer to this entire section (in the above picture) as the user interface, so you might want to take your time and look over everything. Let's log out now, and then find out where to log back in. A gear icon will appear in the top-right corner of your screen. You can use the sign out feature by clicking on it, which will take you back to the screen where you were previously logged in. In order to log back in, go to quickbooks.intuit.com, which is where we were when we initially registered our account, in the search box on Google. When you are ready to log in, click the sign-in notification or choice.

You will register with the specific one to which you are really subscribed, but if you are still using the 30-day free trial without subscribing, simply select the QuickBooks online option, which is the first one as you can see below:

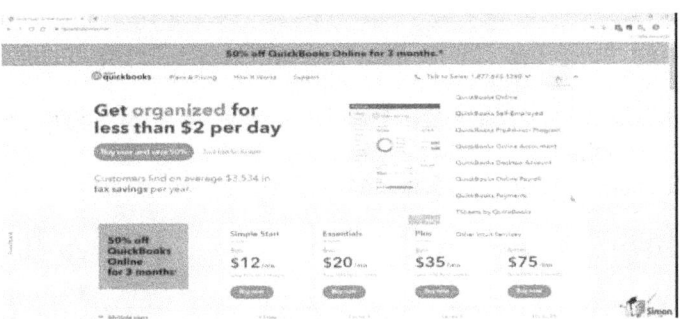

And then that will take you back in and you will be able to log in right over here;

and that is all you need to know right now as far as setting up your company file.

Uploading QuickBooks Desktop File To The Online Version

Here we will be dealing on how to actually go ahead and upload your QuickBooks desktop file if you wanted to bring it into your online account. If you happen to have been using the QuickBooks desktop version and now you would like to pull that data into the online version, there is a little process you need to go through and once you go through the process then, you will want to run reports to make sure that all your data are pulled in. To do that follow the steps below;

1. Open up your company file in the desktop version.

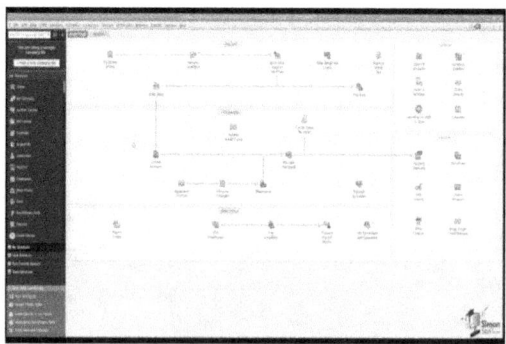

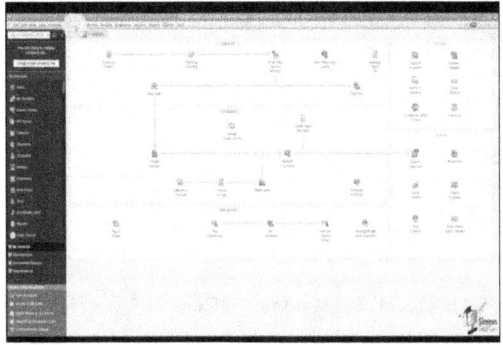

2. Then go to your menu and click on company and down near the bottom you will see export company file to QuickBooks.

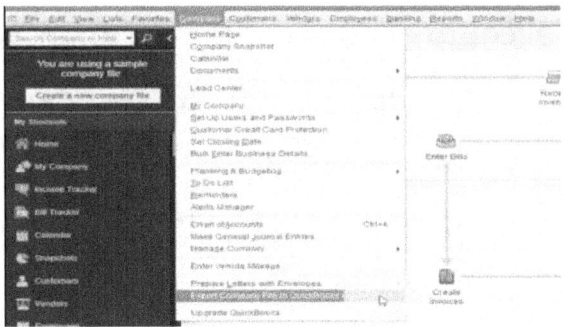

Should that choice be absent, it indicates that there are certain upgrades in this version of QuickBooks that you must complete before exporting can be done.

Simply select Help from the menu, and you will see the option to "Update QuickBooks right here" in the box below.

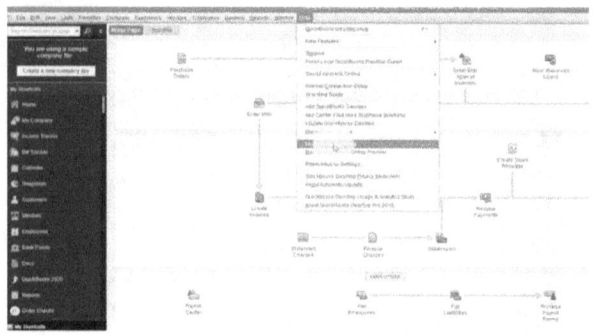

Now, go through that update process and when you are finished, close the company file then open it back up and when you do, you should see the option to export you company file to QuickBooks online. What will happen next is that you will be prompted to log into your online account. You must log in, enter your email address once more (the one you used to register for the online edition of QuickBooks), and enter your password. If, despite your best efforts, it is unable to identify you when you are signed in, it will attempt to send a code to your email address in order to validate your account. After then, you must select the six codes that were delivered to your mail box. However, if you had entered your phone number when creating your account, you might have also received a text message. In any case, insert the plug and press the bottom "continue" button. Before it can really pull it up to the online version, it will ask you a few short questions. Usually, it will inquire whether you would like to bring over your goods. If you answer "yes," you should choose the date you want it to start from and click "continue". Next, it will ask you to select your current QuickBooks online company file. If you have multiple, they will all be listed; simply select the one you want, then click the "Continue" button at the bottom. Right now, Larry's Landscaping and Garden Supply's company file is being prepared. Click OK after exercising patience—this process may take some time. When this procedure is concluded, you will receive an email from Intuit; if you do not receive that email, it is still in progress. Although it may appear to be frozen, it is not; you will receive it eventually. After it is finished, all you need to do is launch the desktop and online versions and compare your data by running various reports in each. It makes no difference which one you work on initially. Thus, we will run balance sheet and profit and loss reports.

As you can see below, click the report, company and financial, profit and loss, standard on your desktop version while it's still in your company file.

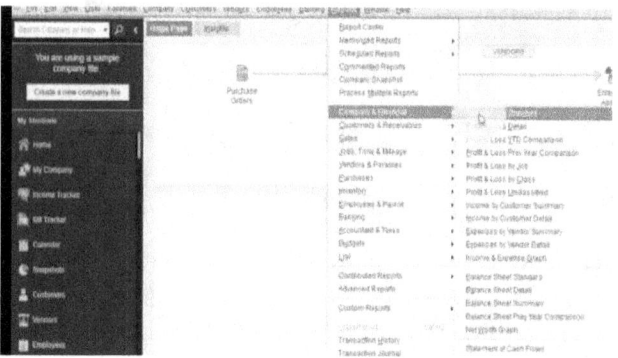

Now, when the report comes up there is a couple things that you need to do. Make sure the dates are in" All", that way you capture everything in your company file. Also make sure you are running this on an accrual basis as below;

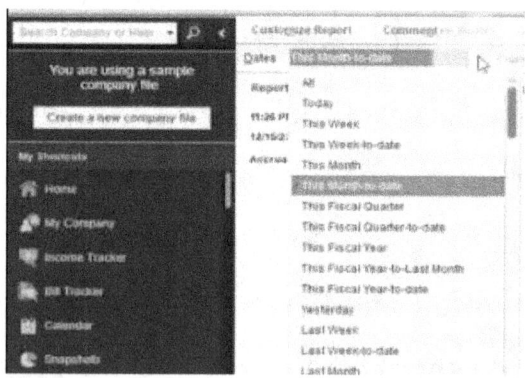

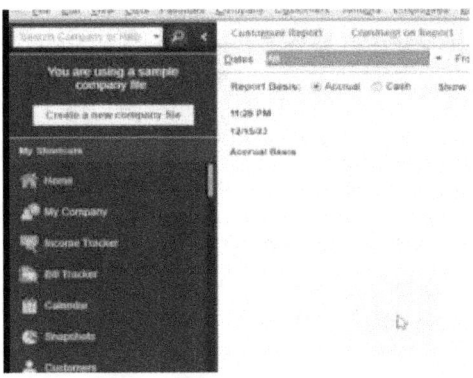

You can also run the balance sheet. You are going to go back to reports, company and financial and run a balance sheet standard make sure that you pick 'All' dates. You will have to scroll up to the top for that and make sure you are running it on the accrual basis as can see underlined with red ink in below picture.

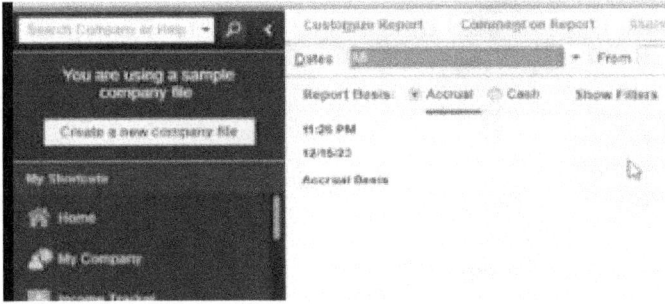

We are using accrual for this report even though, in reality, we would use the cash basis so that you can be sure you have everything.

You can also log in to your online version and retrieve the same reports to verify that they are present and look for any discrepancies.

If you look over here on the left, you can see how to run reports in the online version:

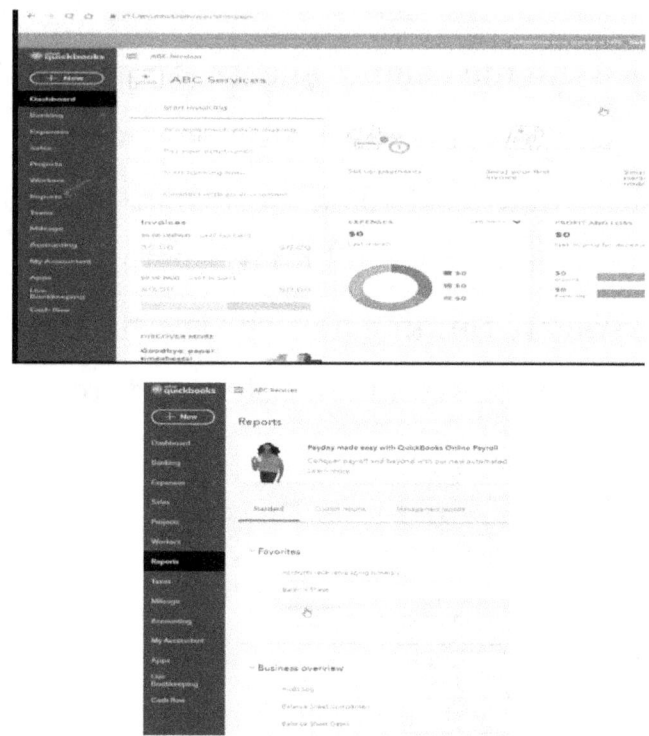

The balance sheet and the profit and loss are automatically placed under your favorites when you click on the reports link (shown by a red arrow). Either one can be run first; it makes no difference. As soon as we begin the profit and loss, and if you receive displays similar to these below,

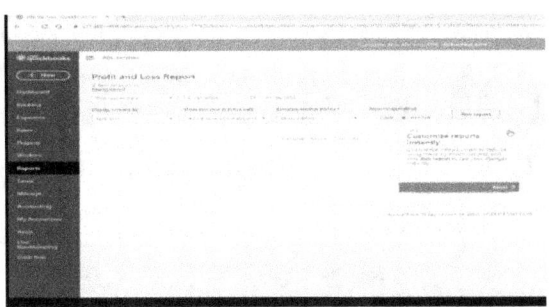

That says customize, go ahead and just close that out for now and what you want to do is make sure that you choose all from the top of the list and then make sure you hit run report and you can see there is the data as you have in your desktop version. You will do the same thing with that balance sheet. You will go back to reports on the Left, you will run the balance sheet.

Make sure that you are running this on accrual basis and also make sure you are looking at the dates 'All' at the top.

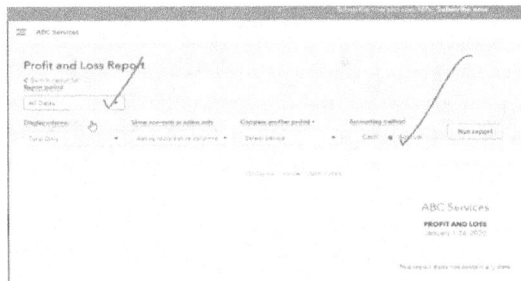

Making sure accrual is selected there, as I mentioned, is essential. After that, you should run your report, print those pages, and compare the two. Should the days be identical on both, then everything is perfectly done; but, if it differs from one day to the next, then it did not truly export all of your data and import it into the online version. In order to transfer your data from your desktop version to your online version, you might want to give it another shot.

Chapter Three

QuickBooks Online User Interface

The QuickBooks Online Dashboard.

Here, we will talk about what's known as the QuickBooks online user interface and provide you with a brief rundown of what it looks like—basically, the screen you see when you load it up—and how each component functions.

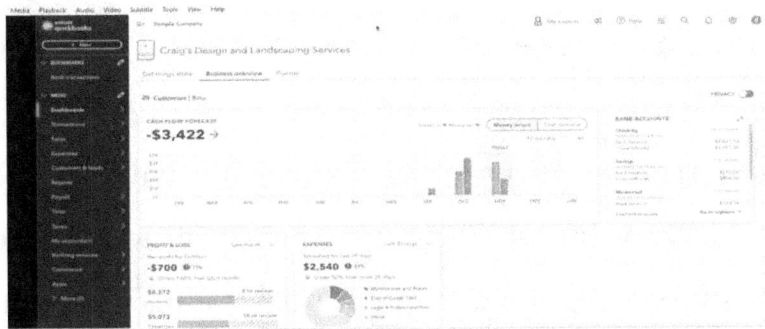

Let's quickly go over everything that is shown on the dashboard. After that, we'll return and highlight what you truly need to know.

1.Company Name Logo

In the top corner, we have your company name and logo. We shall be working with the sample company "Craig's Design and Landscaping Services".

2.Navigation Menu

The gray bar on the left (highlighted yellow) is called the Navigation Menu. You can use this to access different pages and create transactions with the New Button. If you are working on a small screen, you can always hide the Navigation Menu by clicking on this button with the three little Lines indicated with red arrow on the picture below;

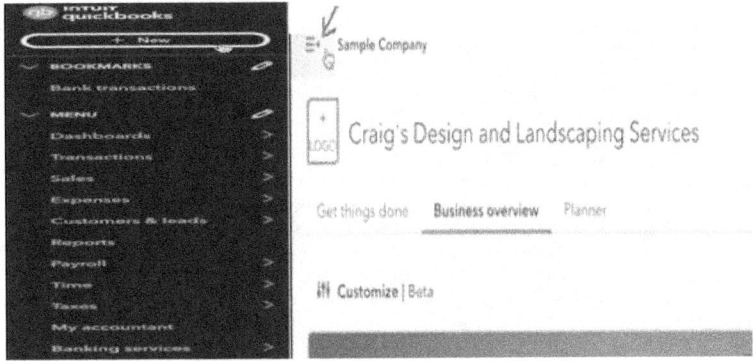

At the top of the Nav Bar we have got the New Button. We can click on this to create new transactions. These are separated into four columns as shown below;

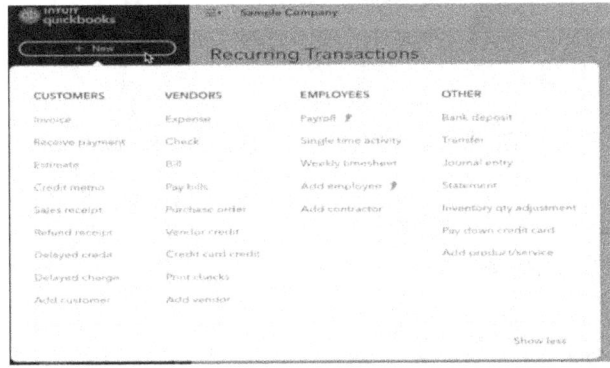

We have Customers, Vendors, Employees and other stuff.

First, let us discuss on how to make an invoice as an example of so many things you can do with the QuickBooks Online. Maybe you have just sold something to a customer. Under customer column, click on invoice and it will display this below;

You can add their name there or pick them from the list. Enter what you

sold them. Change the quantity or rate and then you can apply a discount and add sales tax if necessary. Once you are happy with it click save and

send. QuickBooks Online will create a PDF of your invoice and an email which you can personalize and send to your customer.

This process is almost similar as when you bought something from a vendor. There are two main ways to record a purchase: **Bills and Expenses** (under vendor). If you have already paid then you want to record an Expense. Pick who you paid, the account or credit card that you used (under payment method) add the invoice number (shown as Ref no). Categorize the transaction;

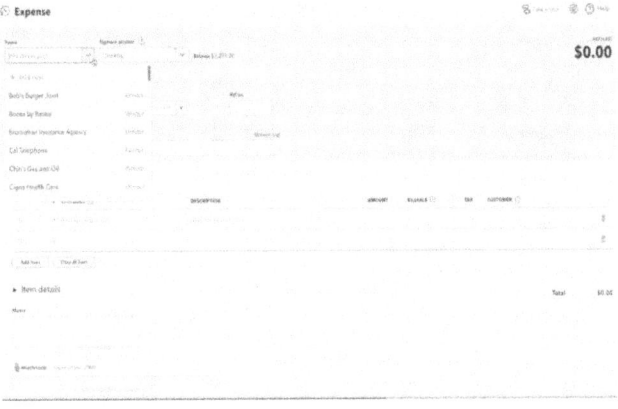

This will change where it shows up in your Income Statement. Enter a description, an amount - you can add more lines if you need to - and then attach a receipt to support the expense, save and close.

QuickBooks also has an app that you can use to photograph and enter receipts on-the-go. In QuickBooks Online we use Bills to record expenses that we will pay at a later date. The form is almost exactly the same, but now we have to add payment terms and a due date as you can see below;

Once you have filled this out you can save the bill and schedule the payment.

On the **Employees column** you can do your payroll and your time sheets.

Other Column:

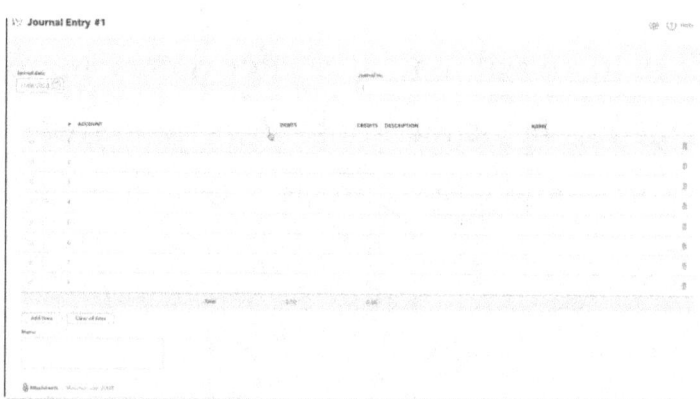

This is where you can create journal entries. If you have got an accountant then you won't want to touch this. But if you are doing it yourself then you can learn all about journal entries before dealing with this column on the app.

Let us head back to the **Navigation Menu**. Under **bookmarks** we have **Bank transactions**;

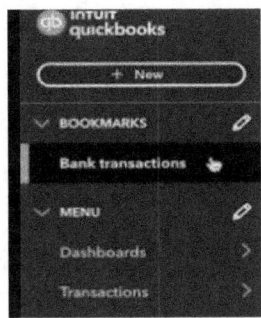

There you can connect your bank accounts and credit cards to QuickBooks Online. This will save you a heap of manual data entry because QuickBooks will automatically download your transactions and populate your bank feed. Which is what we can see below:

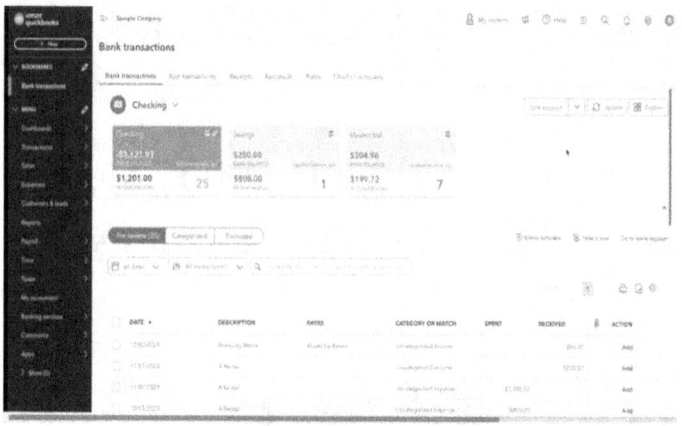

The next step is to do regular bank reconciliations which is a key part of bookkeeping. If a transaction has already been recorded in QuickBooks, then you can drag down the screen and click match to link it to the transaction in your bank feed.

In your bank feed you will also come across uncategorized income and expenses. These transactions have not been recorded in QuickBooks yet. We can add them right there as shown below;

Click on the transaction, select the customer or vendor, pick a category, add a description, attach your support and press add. If you get lots of similar transactions then you can also use Bank rules to categorize them automatically.

Below Bank transactions we have the Dashboard Button which will take us back to the Dashboard. Transactions is for Bank transactions which we touched on already and once it is done, it will be bookmarked.

Sales is the home of your invoices. Here you can keep an eye on your income over time and watch out for any overdue invoices (indicated with red arrow in the picture below). These will be highlighted in a vibrant orange:

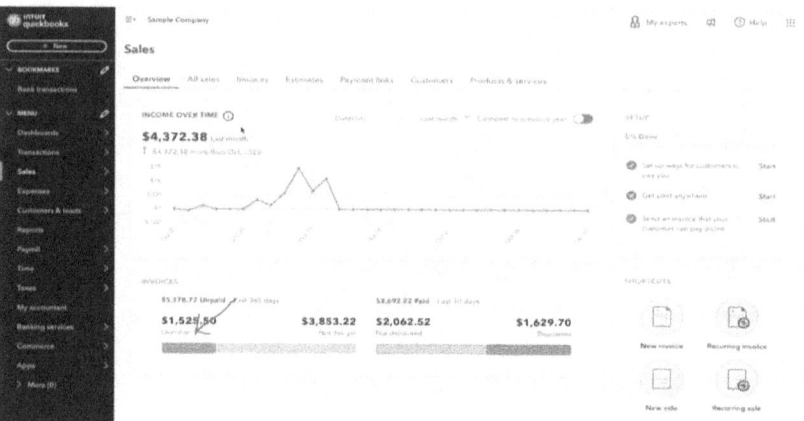

We can click on them to get a list of the culprits and send them reminders via email. This is done when you click on the overdue, it will display list of those whose invoice is overdue to make payment, click Action to send mail to them;

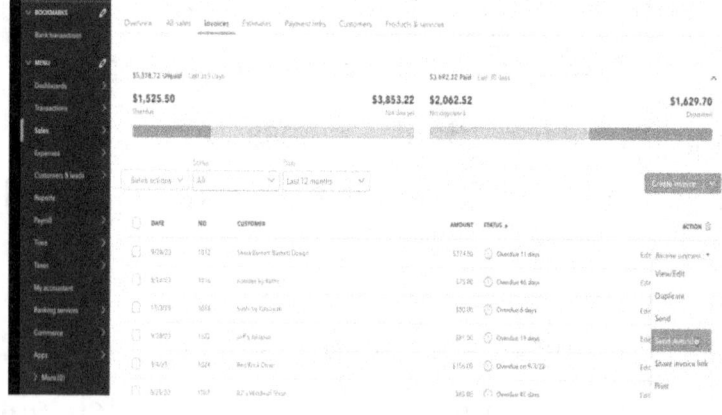

On the Expenses tab we get a list of your business's expense transactions. You can click on Bills to see if anything's overdue. The Vendors

tab will let you add new suppliers and you can track mileage on the Mileage tab. Customers and leads is pretty similar to the Sales tab.

But it also has an interface with MailChimp if you use that. Next up is Reports. We have got all of our favorites at the top. The Balance Sheet is

a Financial Statement that shows your financial position. It provides a snapshot of your Assets, Liabilities and Equity at a point in time.

Then there is the Statement of Profit and Loss also known as the Income Statement. This measures the business's financial performance by summarizing Revenue and Expenses over a period of time. Then, the Cash Flow Statement which is the other main Financial Statement. It lives under Business overview and you can click on the little star to add it to your favorites. The Cash Flow Statement summarizes your cash inflows and outflows over a period of time.

Below Reports we have Payroll. This is where you can manage your employees and contractors.

There is the Time tab which tracks time which can flow through to payroll and invoicing. In Taxes you can manage the business's Sales tax or GST if required.

My Accountant is a workspace where you can invite and talk to your accountant. In Banking services, you can apply for business loans through QuickBooks Capital. You can use Commerce to connect your sales channels like Amazon, eBay and Shopify and in Apps you can add on third party applications to run your business more efficiently.

3. In the top right of the dashboard are; **My Experts, Updates, Help, Apps, the Search button, the Notification Bell, Settings and a link to your Intuit account.**

Business Overview

Let us take a look at the business overview display screen below;

This is the business overview where you can check your Financial Health at a glance. We have summaries of your cash flow, bank balances, profit and loss and expenses (they are all highlighted for you). You can click customize

(highlighted on the left top of the display) to move these summaries around.

If you are working on a train and you are worried about nosy parkers, there is a privacy button (indicate on the above picture with a red arrow) that will hide this sensitive information.

How does QuickBooks Online work?

Let's start with explaining the function of the following buttons shown in the picture below;

A) **My Experts button**: You can use My Experts to connect with your accountant.

b) **Updates**: This gives you short videos and articles outlining the latest changes in QuickBooks.

c) **Help button**: If you are stuck then you can click on the Help button to search through the frequently asked questions. The little **grid of dots** after the help button lets you track your apps and then we have the **magnifying glass** after the grid of dots. This is the Search button. When you click on it you get a list of your recent transactions. Then we have the **Notification Bell** followed by **the gear icon (Which is settings).** If you are new to QuickBooks, you can set your company up by clicking on the setting then go to

Account and Settings and you will have the display below.

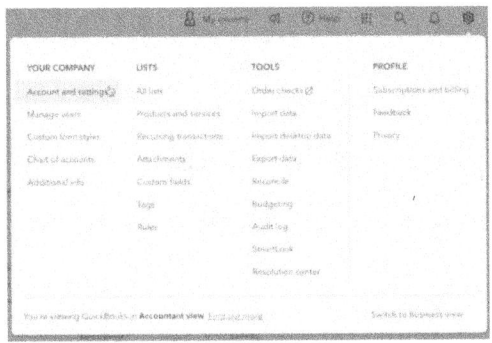

There you can add your logo (by clicking at the point with red arrow) and update your company name. Then for tax you can enter your Employer Identification Number or Social Security Number (EIN or SSN). And moving down you can choose a company type and industry, update your business contact information and add your website.

The panel on the left (indicated with black arrow) lets you check your usage limits, customize your expenses and time sheets. And at the bottom we have Advanced Settings. This is where you can turn on multicurrency if you need it.

Let us hop back into the options you will see when you click on Settings menu.

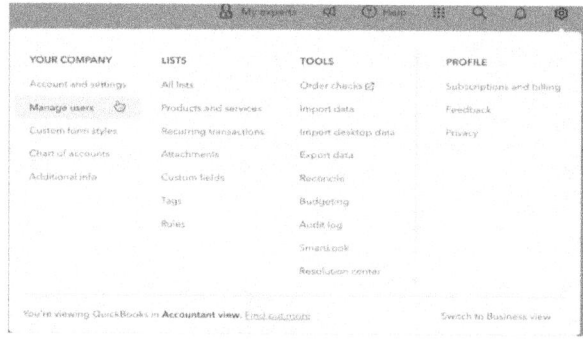

Manage users is where you can add and delete users or change what they have got access to.

Chart of accounts brings up a complete list of your accounts. We use these to sort and store your transactions as shown below

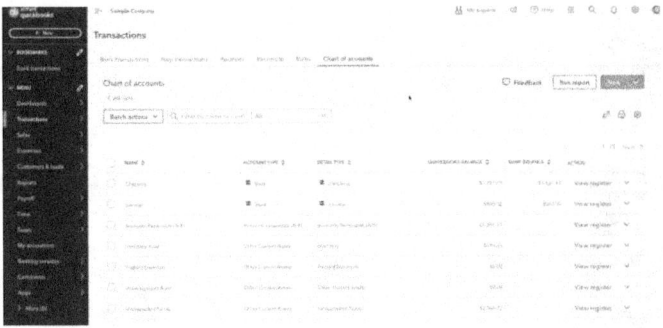

The chart of account will make your life a whole lot easier if you set up your chart of accounts correctly. Every business is different so reach out to an accountant if you need one.

Under **Lists (highlighted below)** you can make changes to the products or services that your business sells.

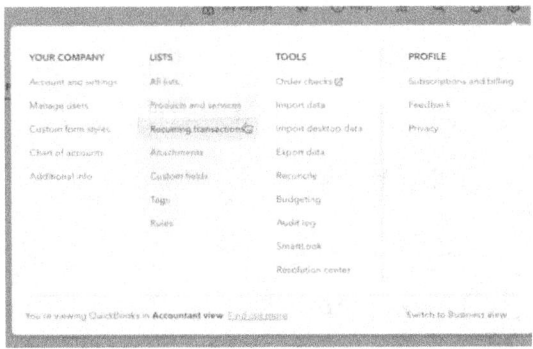

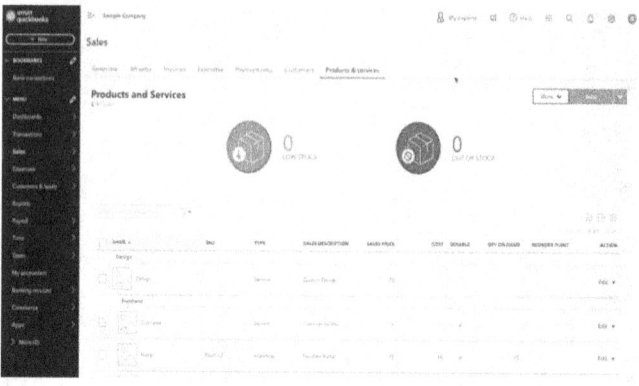

Then there are recurring transactions where you can schedule payments for bills.

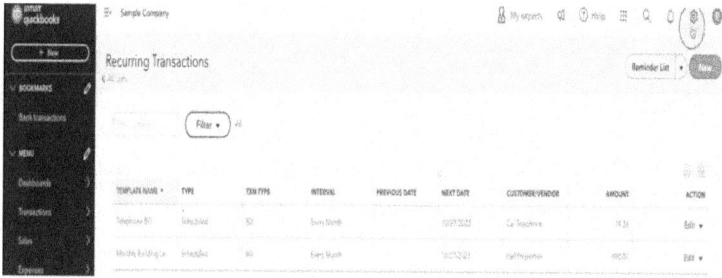

Under Tools you can order checks, import data into QuickBooks, export it. There's a link to reconcile your bank account (which we will talk more on as we progress), you can create a budget, check the audit log to see user activity and then there's SmartLook which is how you share your screen with your accountant. Below is what displays as you click on smartlook.

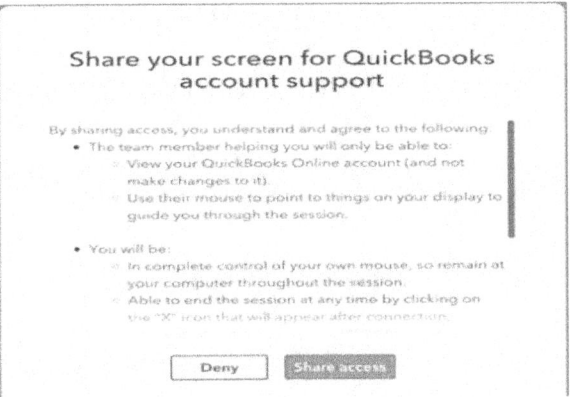

Keyboard Shortcuts.

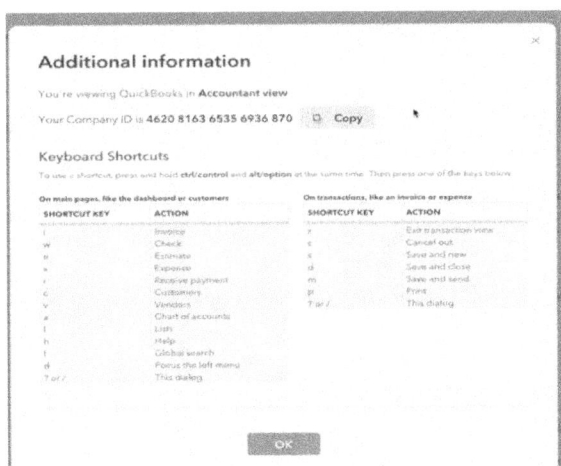

You can find them under Additional info immediately after the chart of account. If you use QuickBooks a lot then these can save you time. I normally write them down and leave them on my desk. You use them by pressing your pad Ctrl +Alt/option at the same time and then press one of the keys on the above picture.

Chapter four

Customizing Your Company File

As we have got familiar with the gear menu, there were lots of different options there that you can use to customize how your company file works and now let us go into the gear menu and into some of those options and show you how to customize some of those different things so that your company file works best for you. As you are still on the user interface, click on the gear icon and we start with the first column underneath where it says your company;

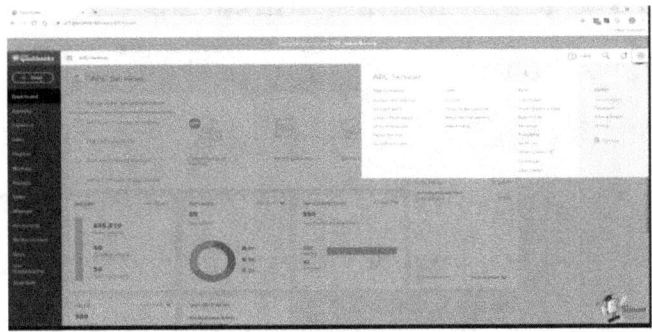

You will see an option that says account and settings and click on it. Those are going to be like preferences or options that you can turn on or off or edit in QuickBooks as we go down the tabs on the left (marked red in the picture below) and we will start with company.

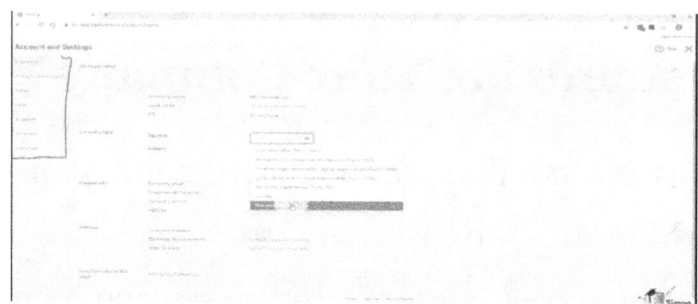

If you want to change anything in these different sections, just go over to the right and click on the little pencil icon and that will take you into the edit option. You will notice there that you can add your company logo just by clicking the plus sign and that will let you navigate through your computer to find your logo. You could edit the name of the company if you like. Also, you might want to put in your EIN number or your social security number. You are going to use your social if you are a sole proprietor and you really do not have payroll. If you do have payroll, you are going to have to have your EIN number in there so that QuickBooks can use it to help you with your payroll and then click save and that will save that little section.

The next little section says company type and you will notice the first thing is the tax form and then the industry. You are going to click over on the pencil icon there and you will notice that you have the ability to add whatever type of tax form that you actually file when you do your taxes at the end of the year. You can add that there. Note, you do not have to pick anything on the tax form section as a matter of fact if you do not file your own taxes, if you have an accountant then you would pick other or none every single time your accountant will know what type of tax form that you file. If you pick any of the other options what will happen is, when you are working in different places in QuickBooks, there will be an extra field that says which tax line on the tax form would you like to put this on. You are not going to have a clue if you are not an accountant and you will just get stuck there every single time. So, why fill that field and get yourself stuck, just pick not sure, other or none.

The other thing you have is an industry you choose when you first set up your company file which you can decide to change if you have another name that best suit your business and hit save.

Next little section you will see there has to do with your company email. You are going to also be seeing your customer facing email. The difference is that, the company email is the private email that you would like different things sent to from Intuit. For example, the customer facing email is the one you want the customer to see and that can actually be redirected to your company email if you do not want to have to open 15 different email accounts. You can always have as many email accounts as you want and redirect them to the one you would like to funnel everything into. There is a place of putting your company phone and your company website there again, you would edit that over on the right and the company address down at the bottom. Same thing, you can have a company address that is seen on the back end and then one that is called customer facing; meaning that is the one that the customer actually sees.

Going down on the left where we mark red on the above picture, you have billing and subscription. This is where you are going to be able to go in and upgrade your existing subscription if you would like. You could notice that you can subscribe right from there and you can see all of the options and as we have talked a little bit about these before.

The next one on the left is usage. There are some limits to some of these different subscriptions for example, when you are using the QuickBooks Online Plus and you need more room. You can go ahead and upgrade your subscription. For instance, the one that am using now only allows me one user. If I want to add a user, I may need to upgrade my subscription. There is a number of items you can put in the chart of accounts as an example, it is 250 just a little fYI. The desktop allows you to have 14,500. If I need 251 then I need to upgrade my subscription.

Down there where it says classes and locations, you can have up to 40 and if you need more, then that is another reason you would want to upgrade your subscription.

We have sales on the left and there are several things in there that you may want to go ahead and work with. When you click on it, it will pop up some things you can turn on or off right there in your forms. For example, let us say that you like to invoice your customers and you want the customers to automatically have terms of net10. You can click on the form net and edit whatever invoice term that is currently on the net to net 10 by clicking on the pencil icon. If you are not familiar with the preferred invoice terms, the ones that say 1% 10 net30, 2% 10Net30, 8% 30 Net 60.

Basically, what that means is that the customer invoice will be due in 30 days but if they paid in 10 days, they can take one percent off. It is a way to get your customers to pay you early. If you have a preferred delivery method you can choose it right here where I marked red in the picture below;

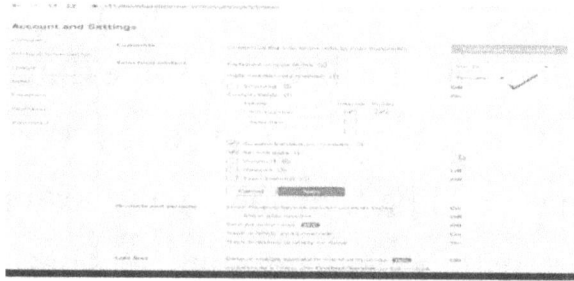

There you will option of; if you like to print things now or would you like to send things later. It is referring to an invoice as an example, there where it says shipping, if you do not ship anything, you uncheck the shipping box and if you do ship things, you mark the box and then you have some options down there where you can have sales reps and put in purchase order numbers (p o), they are custom fields and you can also turn them off if you don't need them. If you want purchase order (p o) number not sales rep for example, just uncheck the sales rep option. You can have custom transaction numbers and that basically means that if you want to put in your own transaction numbers, you can go ahead and set that series up. you can have a service date field; you can also have fields for the discount and deposits or tips or gratuity if you use that. You can just go in and turn them on or off and click save.

The next thing you are going to see is products and services right after the tip (Gratuity) option and when you click it, you will see there are several different options related to that, that you can turn on or off. For example, if you don't track inventory, you turn off the inventory option. There is also, some options for late fees, for progress invoicing and let us touch on what that is just so you will know. If you estimate jobs construction (a prime example), you are going to want to take that estimate and turn it into an invoice at some point so that your customer can pay you. You do not have to pull everything from the estimate into an invoice, you can pull in 30% for example, or maybe you want to pull in certain items that were on that estimate into an invoice. If you do estimates, you will want progress invoicing. Scroll down for a couple more options there. For messages when you actually email a form. So, let us say it is an invoice for example or what they call a sales form, you have the ability to email it directly to your customer. You can set the default message. When you click on it, you have many default messages that will pop up and you will go ahead and click on one of your choices and notice you have beside it, more field for full name if you want to have their full name. There is lastname, firstname and you can use the standard message that you see right there below. When you are actually sending out that email you can also have a copy email to yourself every time if you care by checking the box for it and hit save. Also, there is an option for reminders which when you click the pencil icon, there is a couple of options that you want to be familiar with. You have the ability to set up invoice reminder emails. For an example, if your customer is late paying an invoice or you just need for some reason that you want to remind your customer to pay that invoice, you either use the standard message or you can go ahead and edit the one that you see down there which says 'this is a reminder we haven't received your payment yet'. You do have the ability to insert a placeholder which basically means that anywhere in there, you can put in the company name or the invoice number and that would actually be a merged transaction as what they call it;

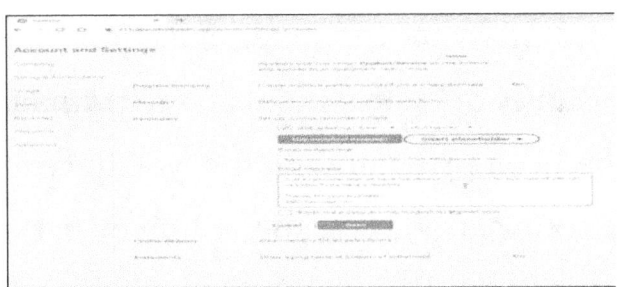

It will pull from QuickBooks that information. You can email yourself a copy and hit save.

Down there at the bottom, there is option for online delivery. These are email options for all of your sales forms. Your options for this will be when you actually email your sales form over to your customer, you may probably want to have a short summary show up in the email or show the full details in the email. You can also attach it as a PDF right there and some additional options you have is, if it's an online invoice you can actually set it up for HTML or if you want it to show up in plain text but you probably want to leave it (as online invoice) and then click Save.

The last one is statements; a statement goes out at the end of the month and basically it starts with the balance from the prior month. It shows all of the transactions that month and then what the customer owes at that point. It is really a gentle reminder for your customer to go ahead and pay you. Statements are not mandatory but they certainly do help when you are trying to collect money. When you print statements, you have an option to list each transaction on a single line or list each one including all the details on that particular one. You can also show the aging table at the bottom of the statement and what that means is, it will have a field that says one to thirty days, another one that says 31 to 60 and another says 61 to 90 and that way, your customer will know where they fall in that particular aging table. After all that is set, click save. With this, you are done with options on sales.

The expense option. Expenses are something you must pay for; bills you receive in the mail are one example. You can choose to have the item table displayed on the purchase and expense forms. You have the ability to bill customers for costs and things, track costs and items by customer, and set default conditions for bill payment. Making expenses in goods chargeable suggests that, should you need to buy a good or service, you should make sure to bill your client so you may get paid back. Instead of just manually putting those receipts in the car or keeping them on your desk, QuickBooks will remember those expenses and when you are ready to invoice the customer you can just pull them in. You also have the ability to use the purchase order system but can uncheck the box if you do not need it. Also, you have this option called messages at the bottom. This is a default message that will be sent when you send purchase orders, click if you wish to see the default message which you can also edit to say anything you like and then make sure you save it when you are done.

Payments is the next tab under Account and Settings. This is related to receiving payment from a client. There are two options available to you. The first is using QuickBooks' small service to register in order to receive payments more quickly. It functions remarkably similarly to zel or PayPal. to make use of this service, or click the learn more button.

If you use this service, you can email an invoice to a customer, for example, and they can pay you immediately away by clicking a button; QuickBooks will update automatically as soon as you get payment from your customer. If you already have some sort of existing account with Intuit for example, they have something called go payment or merchant services you can connect it to your QuickBooks as well right there (indicated with red arrow in the picture below)

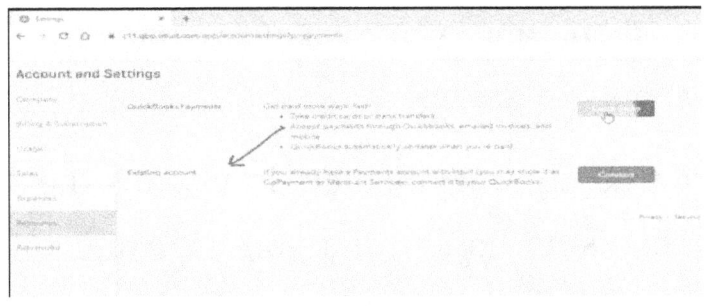

The last option says **advanced.** There are several things you can do with this option. For instance, if you want to have the first month of your fiscal year start maybe in September, you can affect that by changing the default month which is January and make it correspond with your real existing started or fiscal year. You might have a different date for the beginning of your income tax year and you also change that.

You have accrual selected as your accounting method. You have the option of running reports on a cash basis or an accrual basis. In essence, accrual refers to the fact that your invoiced amount appears as income regardless of whether your clients have paid you. Whether or whether you have paid a bill, it will appear when you record it as an expense. If you switch it to what is known as a cash basis, you will only be able to display your income once you have received payment from the client and your expenses once you have actually spent the money.

Below the accounting method is closing the books option. This is an option that you will want to think about. In real life accounting, you close the books at the end of the month and you close the books at the end of the year. What that means is, if you want to make a change in a closed period you cannot do it, you need to make an offsetting entry in the current period. Your books are not closed automatically in QuickBooks. It does not remind you anything. So, if you want to close them you have to come to the closing books option and there you will be able to tell QuickBooks that you do want to close the books and then you can set a closing date of your choice. For example, if you set it for December 31 of 2023 that means that after you are working in the next year but you see a change you want to make in 2023 prior to December 31, you are not going to be able to change it. So, to be able to effect any change anytime, you should leave that off.

Next on the advanced option is the chart of accounts, basically everything in QuickBooks will run through this chart of accounts and currently they do not have general ledger numbers, they are just a list alphabetical for each type. If you want to turn on general ledger numbers you can turn them on right there. You also have some options for the markup income account and we will address that a little bit later. The track classes and the track locations. locations means if you have different physical locations for your business, you can turn this option on and every transaction that you work on, you can choose which location you want that to go to. Classes is very similar except it is not really locations. For example, let us say that you happen to have two different divisions of your company, you might use those for your class list and everything you do make sure you pick the correct option from the list. There are some things about forms where you can have it pre-fill automatically, automatically apply payments that you might want to look through at some point.

A project would be like a job-related activity. Here, you have the ability to organize all of those job-related activities in one place and that is turned on. You are also viewing QuickBooks in the business view, if you want to change it, click the view and there is an option to change it accountant view. **Time tracking;** if you want to be able to track the time that you or your employees spend working on different projects or jobs, you have the ability to do that and you can also come down and change the currency. There is some date options and things like that all the way down. There are lots of options you can go through and set. You are going to want to look through them and may not want to set them all right away but at some point, if you want to set them, you just come back in and make all these changes. You can close this interface with the X at the top right and that will bring you back to the dashboard.

Managing Users

One of the things that you will want to do is make sure that each person that is using QuickBooks has their own login. You will give each person their own username and their own password. Only the administrator can add, edit or delete users. You can have up to five users in your QuickBooks file. If you need additional ones you can think about upgrading your subscription or purchasing those additional ones that you might need. The reason you want to have these additional users set up is because, if you want to track down the errors then, you will want to know who was logged in at the time that particular transaction was changed. You can run an audit trail to see a report on which user was logged in, what the transaction used to look like and what it looks like now. You also will be able to limit the users access to certain areas of QuickBooks. keep in mind that the administrator has to be logged in; in order to work with the users. To set this up, follow the below steps;

Click on the gear icon in the top right-hand side of the screen and in the first column, you will see an option that says manage users.

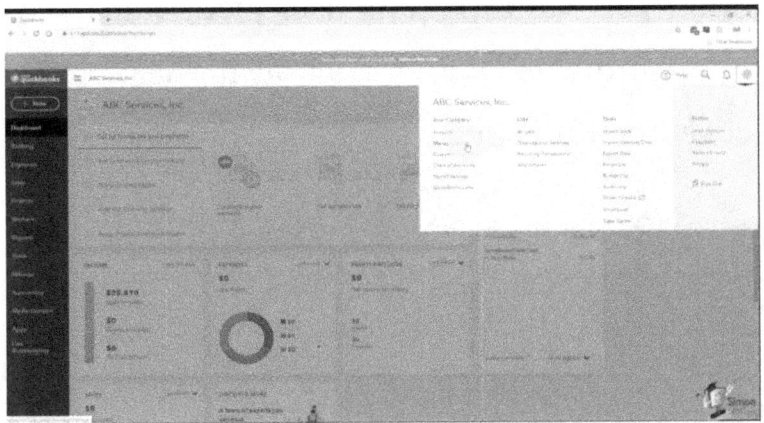

Normally, if you are using one of the basic subscriptions then, you only have five of what they call billable users in your plan and like I mentioned earlier you do have to upgrade if you want to have additional users. The admin is considered one of the five users and when you click on the manage users, the admin name is the first name on the screen that will be displayed and if you wanted to edit the admin information, you can choose the Edit over on the right and then you can now edit it on the user settings that will be displayed. Typically, when you first set up QuickBooks you are going see the email address that you signed up with right there under the first name field and there won't be anything where it says last name. You could come up there and change it and click save

At the bottom if you want to add a user just come over to the right there indicated with red arrow in the picture below and click on add user.

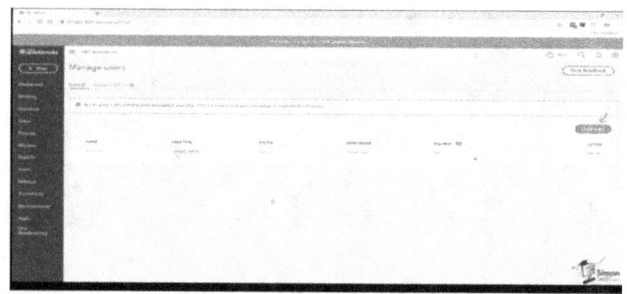

Your User that you are setting up can have what they call standard rights which means that, you can choose to give them full rights but you can also choose to limit their access to certain areas. You may choose to give them company admin rights which means they have access to everything.

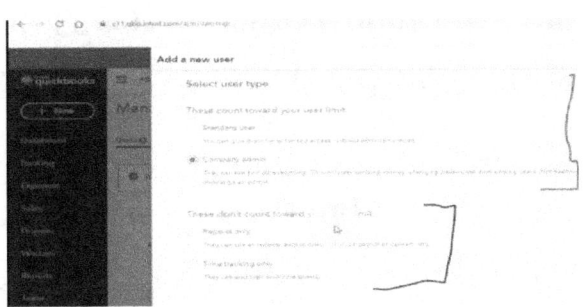

These options up there (select red) count towards your five-user limit we discussed while those below (selected blue) don't because you might have someone you want to be able to log in just to run reports or maybe just to do time tracking. So, you can click on standard user (since you already have admin user) and click Next in the bottom (right-hand corner) of the screen. The first thing it will asks you is how much access do I want to give this user. If you say all, you will notice it will include payroll and it will check the box for it and you can see all the different things they have access to over at right hand side of the screen. If I go ahead and uncheck the payroll box, you will notice that the things they don't have access to do will be down at the bottom with red X sign (they can't add or edit employees in this case or delete payroll transactions). If you check the none box instead, it means that you don't want them to have rights to any of those accounting features but they can still manage other things in QuickBooks like submitting their own timesheets and things like that. You can decide to check the limited access option (and also check the customer box below it) if you want them to be able to do things with customers and you can see the choices of what the user can do with customer will be displayed. if you also want them to do things with vendors or both (vendor and customers), you can check both and you will see all the options on the screen and then hit next. It will ask you if you want this user to "add edit and remove users" we are going to say no because you want the administrator to have rights to everyone. If you start giving everyone full rights to change users and that sort of thing then, it becomes pointless setting those up. Below you notice you can grant the user permission to add company information and also manage subscriptions. After you check or uncheck the boxes depending on the permission you want to grant the user, you then click next at the bottom then it says "we will invite them to create a QuickBooks account and password for each to access the company file". What is required here is for you to put the new users' first and last name there, put in their email and they will actually get an email saying that the administrator would like them to become a user. They would accept and then they can set up the username and password. Make sure that the administrator knows that information, you wouldn't want to have an employee that has their own username and login information and the administrator is not privileged to that information and cannot have access to what they do which is very important. Then click X button. At this point what would happen is, once they accept it, you would see their name as one the users.

The Chart Of Account

The chart of accounts is probably the most important thing in QuickBooks. Every single thing in QuickBooks will flow through the chart of accounts somewhere. The chart of accounts is basically a listing of different areas where you might actually spend money or you might receive money as well and you will want to make sure that your information goes into the correct categories and that way when you run reports you have accurate information. There are a few different ways to get to the chart of accounts; one way is to go through the gear icon and in the first column you will see the chart of accounts;

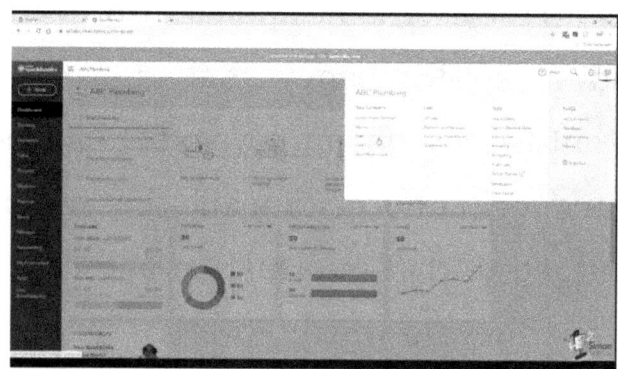

Another way is just go over to the left and click on accounting and there you will see the chart of accounts as well:

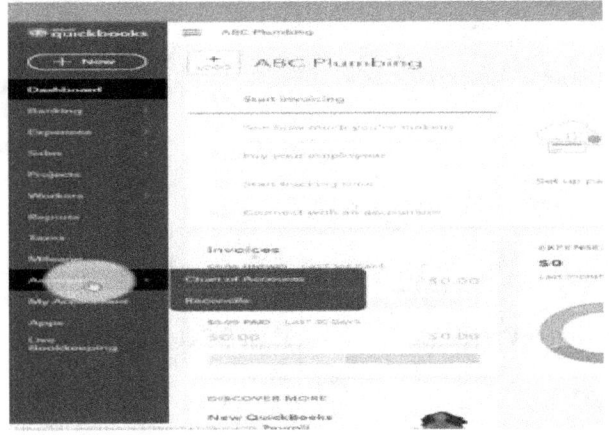

Below is what your chat of accounts looks like:

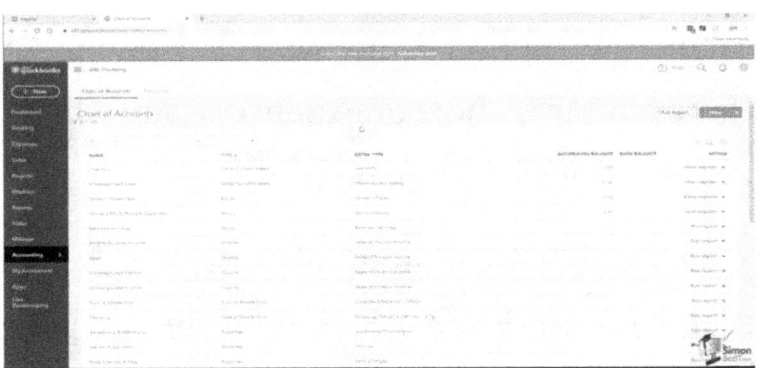

Remember that every single thing in QuickBooks runs through one of these and that is why it so important that this is set up correctly.

The Screen Overview Of The Chart Of Account

The first column is the name of your account. When you are setting these up, you can pretty much name these accounts anything you would like but make sure that you name them something that makes sense to you or whoever happens to be looking at your reports. The second column is the type and notice that it is currently sorted by type. We will be looking at each type so that you will know which ones you need to set up to make sure that you have everything you need. The second column is the type of account sorted alphabetically, followed by the detail type, next is QuickBooks balance, bank balance and action. When you click on any of the types (for example income or expenses), you will notice that they are all sorted alphabetically.

To turn on general ledger numbers you have the option to do that, click on the gear icon then you are going to go into account and settings, choose advanced on the left-hand side and under advanced you see an option that says "enable account numbers" right there. If it is off, click on the off and a dialogue will give you option to put that on and you check the box that says enable account numbers and that of "show account numbers" then save.

When you close and come back to your chart of account screen, you notice that you will have a new column at the beginning where you can actually go through and putting your own account numbers (Below is a sample of the chart of account window);

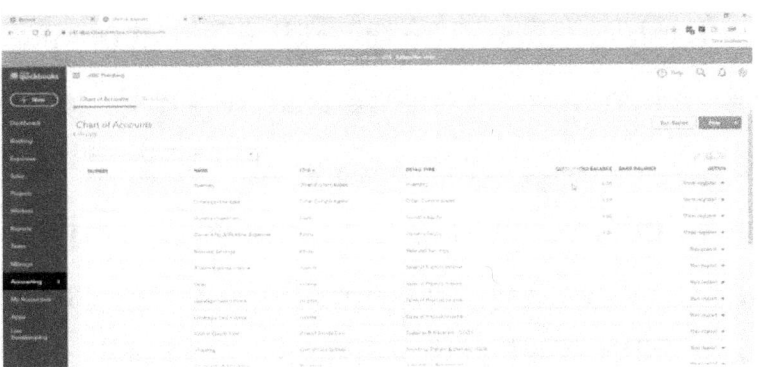

They will not be in there automatically; you have to add them. The way you would add them is the way you would edit any of the accounts. To edit or add the account number, just come over to that line that the account you want to edit is on, under action column you will see "view register" click the down arrow and choose edit and it bring up a window where you have the opportunity to add your new account number or edit the already existing one if you had added one before. You can go back on the same process you went by clicking on the gear icon, select advanced option, turn off enable account number and uncheck the box for show account and hit save.

On the next column which is "Detail type". This is just telling you a little bit more information about the type that you chose. There is also the QuickBooks balance and the bank balance. The QuickBooks balance would be, if you had entered some transactions in QuickBooks what is that balance for that account. The bank balance column will allow you, if you pull in your entries from the bank (that is called downloading your transactions) then, you will see what that balance is as well and you can see that you can match them up and see if you are in sync there.

Let us discuss a bit on the different types of accounts you'd want to add and have a look on how it works.

The first type is the bank accounts; you will notice that under the account type, there are no bank accounts at the top of the list and that means that right now, you do not have a checking account, you do not have a savings account or any kind of bank account. You have the ability to add them. You will do this by clicking on "New" over there at the top right hand, click on the arrow down on line of and pick bank. When you click it. notice all the other types aside the bank and we shall talk on them as we progress. Next, click on detail type and pick the option from the list that closely matches the account type you intend to create. By the right is the name of the account where you name your account. You can name it anything that best defines the account like; operating account, payroll account or whatever you like to name it. Below is description which is totally optional and you notice there is no sub account right now but later on we will talk about how sub accounts work. The next thing is to scroll down and choose a start date to start tracking the money in that account. Your options are to pick; the beginning of year (say first January), beginning of this month, today or other. The reason you might want to pick "other" is, what if you have a bank statement that cuts off in the middle of the month that would be an option where you can tell it a specific date to start with. It really does not matter what date you start with just try to make it correspond to the start date of your bank statement. Let for instance choose other n put beginning of this year and put in the balance. The ending balance on 23/31 of 2023 would be the exact same number as the beginning balance of 1/ 1/ 2024. It is best you get that number from your bank statement. You can for example, put 500 dollars and 83 cents, hit save and close at the bottom.

Now on top of your chart of account, you will see the account you set being on the chart of account with exact details and figures as you created and set it to be. You also have the ability to view the register. View the register to see if the checkbook register actually looks alike. And if you want to go back to chart of account screen, just click where it says "go back to the chart of account" on top of the register as indicated with a blue arrow on the picture below;

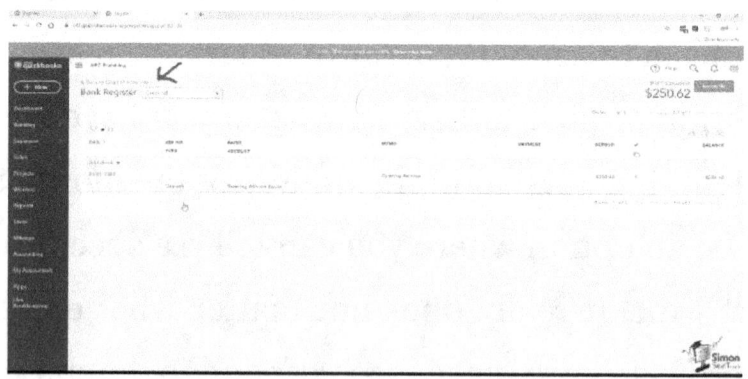

Notice something that happened on your chart of account; Anytime in accounting you do something like what we did, then you will have a debit and a credit for that transaction. You will notice that in this case, the flipside of the money went to an account called opening balance equity and that is the way it should be. You cannot change that, just know that whenever you have a starting balance which could be a minus number if you have a loan.

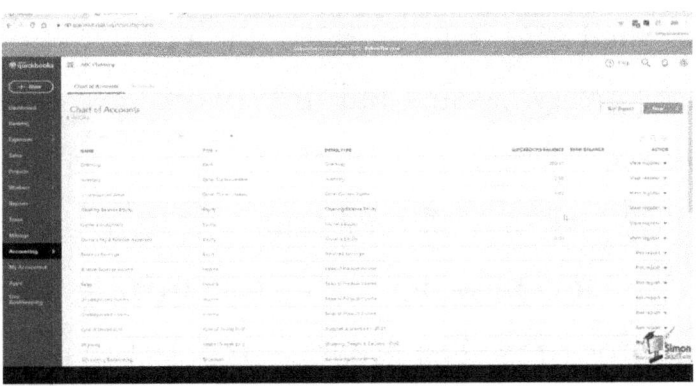

Above is the actual picture of what your books look like. So, do not freak out if you see a negative number there, it is an accurate picture of your books.

We have some other bank accounts; you obviously would have savings, money market accounts and things like that but think about do you have PayPal, do you accept square those are bank accounts as well. So, if you do accept those then you want to set them up as bank accounts. What would eventually happen is, you would transfer money from PayPal or square into your checking account or sometimes you go the other way but those are just bank transfers.

The next type are your assets and you can see there are a couple of it there on the chart of account. An asset is something that your business owns that makes it more valuable such as; equipment, chairs, desk, lamps, vehicles property. Assets fall into two types; there are **fixed assets** (which are things you plan to keep for long-term) like the vehicle or property, then the **liquid assets** which QuickBooks calls "**other current asset**" an inventory is a great example of that. All you need to do assets is to set up big bucket categories and what that means is, instead of listing each vehicle the business owns, you will have a category called vehicles and they will be listed under that one category. Needless having lots of different categories for your assets because no one wants to sit there and look at that, just have big buckets maybe seven to ten good ones. Some of the common ones that I see are: vehicles, furniture and fixtures, property and if you have a lot of property, you might have equipment, but again they are just big buckets. This is where the accountants are going to be very helpful to you because the accountant is going to help you decide which categories to set up and also when you start talking about the money part, then the account is going to help you plug in how much the vehicles were worth and depreciation. QuickBooks does not do depreciation and that is because there are multiple ways to do it if you had ten accountants, they might all tell you a different way they want it done. So, just have the account set up so that if you go to the bank to get a loan for example, the bank will know that you do have some assets.

Setting the liabilities account. A liability is something you owe but not monthly payments you have to pay like the electric bills etc. Here we have things like loans. There are two types; the long term (which are things that you are going to pay on for more than 12 or 13 months), then there is short term (which is under a year basically) and QuickBooks calls them other current liabilities. When you set up your liabilities, you may set up a separate one for each loan that you have and these loans could be a car loan, it could be you as the owner decide to set up a loan where you put money into the business and you want to get paid back. You might have borrowed from the bank. Those are all different liabilities you could set up and each one should be set up separately. As demonstration, let us set up a car payment so you can get an idea of how you would set up these accounts: Click on new and the first thing it asks you is to pick the account type, there you are going to see your other current (which is a short term) and your long-term liabilities (which what you are to choose in this case).

Under detail type, you will see notes payable which is basically accounting term for loan. By your left of the set-up dialogue screen your see "name", there you type the name you want for the loan so that you can see which loan you are looking at when you have to pulled it up (let just put bank of any city as the name of the loan). Next is description which is totally optional. That is where you might say that this is my 2023 highlander loan or you can leave it blank and then you are going to pick a start date. Remember, if you are starting your company at the beginning of the year, what you will do is that, for your beginning balance there, find out what the amount you owed as of in this case January 1, so that you can plug that in. It is not the amount you started with when you purchase the vehicle a years ago, it is the amount you owed as of the start date of your company file, I'm going to put $15,000 and then hit save and close at the bottom.

On the chart of account below;

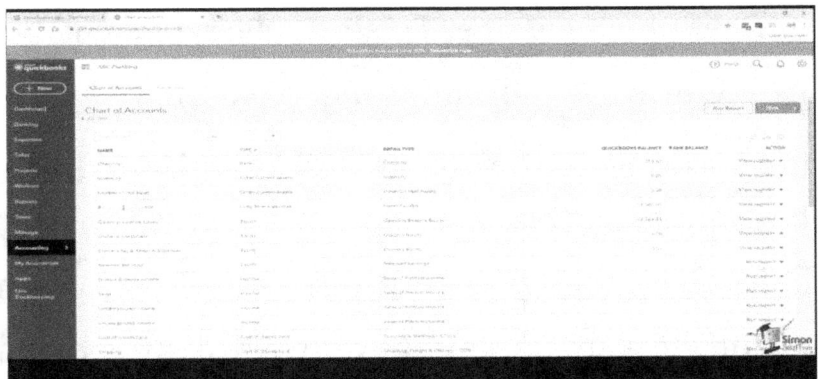

You will   see that you have a loan right there. Notice it says Bank of any city and the balance is $15,000. Every time you make a payment on the loan that is the account you have to put it to. Your car payment is not an expense to the business, do not set it up as an expense account. It is a loan and you want to know when you have paid off the loan. You will also notice that your opening balance equity is on negative number and that is because I said that when you owe something, it will be a negative number and that is an accurate picture of what your books look like.

On setting up credit cards, these are credit cards that your business uses to purchase items for the business. This has nothing to do with accepting customer credit cards. You may want to set each credit card account up separately so that you can track each one. Let us as a practice set up a new one. To start, click new, the type will be credit card and under name, you may name it say "visa" and pick the start date of your company file, the beginning of this year and the starting balance would be the starting balance from my January bank statement. If you do not have your January bank statement then you can grab your December of 2023 and plug that number in. Maybe you say was $2,500 and hit save and close. On your chart of account, you will see i that you have a credit card and you owe $2,500 when you make a payment towards the credit card, you are going to actually put it to that account always.

Next, the type that I want to mention is where you see equity. Equity basically means equal. If you think about it, you are the owner of the company. When you take money out, that's considered an owner draw. When you put money in, it is considered an owner contribution. Now, they have got some other terminology. You will notice owner investment is when the owner puts money into the business, and personal expenses are when the owner takes money out of the business. What you do not do is, you do not make a deposit from your personal account and consider it income. It is not income to the business; it's considered equity.

The next type that I want to talk to you about are your income accounts. Just a little bit here;

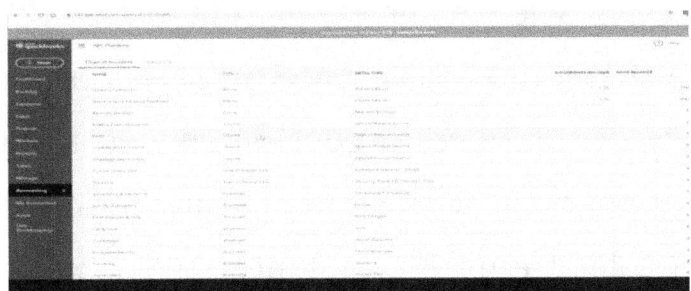

On the above picture, you are going to see that there is one called sales income. Typically, when you make a sale for your business, this is the account that you want your sales to dump into. You can have a few extra ones added if you would like. Maybe you have different areas that you do business in. What I mean by that is in your company, maybe you have different things that you do, and you will want to set those up so you can see how much income you are getting from each one. That is certainly okay. Keep that list pretty short, though; no one wants to read 50 different lines of income accounts. But sales are normally where you will see most of that go into.

The next thing I want to mention is your cost of goods sold. Think about the things that you have to buy to make a product or service in your business. You have to buy materials; you are going to need subcontractors sometimes, maybe you have freight that is part of that. Anything that you have to buy to make a product or service in your business is considered a cost of goods sold, and you want it to show up on a profit-loss as being deducted from your total income.

The largest grouping that you are going to see are your expense accounts, and you will notice there are a ton of it here below;

To add some sub-accounts using car and truck as an example. We have the main account on the chart indicate in the picture with a red arrow, but I want to add a sub-account called gas and maybe another one called repairs and maintenance. All you are going to do is go back up to the new option in the top right of your screen. There, you are going to create a new account, and it has to be the same type as the main account. So that means that under account name, you put expense, on detail type it will be auto, under name in this case, I want to name it fuel and then check it as a sub-account by checking the sub-account box, and then from the list there, you can pick car and truck (with this, that fuel is a sub-account of car and truck). When you click Save and close at the bottom, you will see how sub-accounts look. On the chart of account, you can see how fuel looks like, it is indented a little bit? That's a sub-account, and there's going to be a lot of sub-accounts you may want to add when you go down list of account on your chart.

Think about insurance; you might have general liability; you might have auto insurance; those would be sub-accounts of insurance going down under legal and professional fees. Often what you will see is accounting and the attorney will be sub-accounts of legal and professional fees. You can just come down and make this list look any way you want.

There are utilities at the bottom; you will want to have telephone underneath, gas, electric, any of the utilities that the business pays. That is going to give you a quick overview of setting up your chart of accounts. Make sure you spend some time on this and get it set up the way you want it. You want it to be as detailed as you need it to be to get your numbers, but do not make it so detailed that no one wants to read it.

You can always go through all we have talked on this chart of account and set up the accounts later because if you are not able to catch up with all right away. Well, at this point we wrap up the chart of accounts.

Chapter five

Accounts Receivable

We will be talking a little bit about the accounts receivable portion of QuickBooks. If you are not familiar with that term, anything happening to do with customers in your business, that is called accounts receivable. Customers are people or businesses that buy from you. You are typically going to make a sale, and that is going to be income to your business. We need to talk first of all about how the customer list is set up, and then once we do that, we will go into the second section, and I will show you how to add some customers to this list.

The way you are going to get to a list of your customers is to go over to your navigation bar on the left, point to sales, and then you will see customers in the list at the very top of your customer list. There, you can see the dollar amount for any of these categories below;

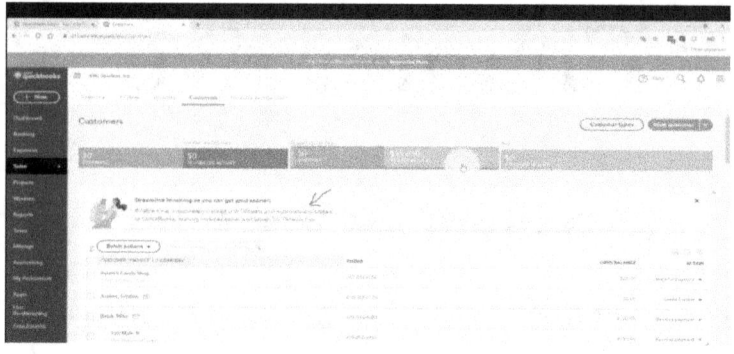

You can see that for open invoices, I have thirty-five thousand eight hundred and ten dollars. These are invoices that have been created, and the customer has not paid them. Even if they owe a penny, if you had any of this amount that was overdue, you would see that over there. Overdue means that if you had set specific terms on an invoice, say net 30, meaning that invoice was due in 30 days, and the customer has not paid you by then, then some of those on open invoice moves over into the overdue category. You can also see how much was paid in the last 30 days (under the paid column) and in this case, nothing. There is also a dollar amount for what we call unbilled activity and for estimates. Sometimes you will get little messages like you see (where I indicated with a red arrow on the above picture) right above your actual customer list. You can close those with the little X in the right-hand corner, and then you can actually see the list.

The customer list is set up alphabetically by last name. You will notice that when you look down the list, the list is set up by last name comm first name. You will want to do that because it is a lot easier to find someone when you are looking for them if it is set up that way. Obviously, a business like (Adams Candy Shop) would not have a last name and a first name, so it just sorts the first letter, which is A in this case with the A's in the list. If you see a little envelope to the right of some of your customers, that means that if you click there, you can actually send that customer an email. If their email address was set up when you actually set up the customer, then it would pull it. If not, you are going to notice that there is no envelope, meaning that you have not put in a customer email address in the customer information.

There are what we call sub-customers below the customers. Sometimes they are called jobs, sometimes they are called projects. For this online version, the technical term is a sub-customer. They are both sub-customers of, in this case, Mike Ballack. You can also see the customer's phone number and the open balance, meaning how much money that customer owes you. There is also a column for actions. If you happen to be on this screen and you would like to take one of these actions related to this customer, you could do that. For example, you can go ahead and create a statement or an invoice right from there.

Notice you can also search for a customer right up there with magnifying glass insignia. So, if you wanted to look for Mike Billick, for example, you can start typing the last few characters of their name, and then you will see that it pops up in the list. Over on the right-hand side, you have the ability to print a list of your customers. You can also export this list to Excel if you like, and there's also some settings. I want to click on the settings for a moment because I want to show you the columns that you see there;

If you like to see their email address, you just choose that from the column and you notice having email column on the list. Or if you like to see their address, you can click on that, and now you see their address as well. It's just how do you want to actually look at this list?

Another thing I want to mention is way back over in the left where it says batch actions. If you have multiple customers selected by checking their box, from the drop-down list when you click on the batch action, you can actually email all selected customers, or you can make them inactive. An inactive customer is a customer you have used in the past; therefore, you can't delete them. But if you have not seen them in a long time and you just want to hide them from the list, you can make them inactive. That's a quick overview of the screen itself here;

How To Add A Customer To The Customer List

Now that you gotten a quick overview of what the customer list looks like and how it works, we need to start adding some customers to your list of customers.

If you are in your customer list, you will notice in the top right-hand corner, there is an option to add a new customer.

There is also a down arrow to the right of that because you can also choose to import customers. With a quick overview of what the customer list entails and how it functions, it is time to populate it with some customers. Transitioning to QuickBooks, I will guide you through the process of adding your initial customer.

In the top right corner of your customer list, you will find the option to "Add a new customer." There's also a dropdown arrow, offering the choice to import customers, particularly useful if you have already compiled a customer list in Excel.

As we begin, just click on **new customer**. The initial input required is the company name. Remember, a customer entry can represent either a company or an individual affiliated with a company. If it is an individual without a company association, simply leave the company name field blank. In this demonstration, I will input the company name as BRC Supplies.

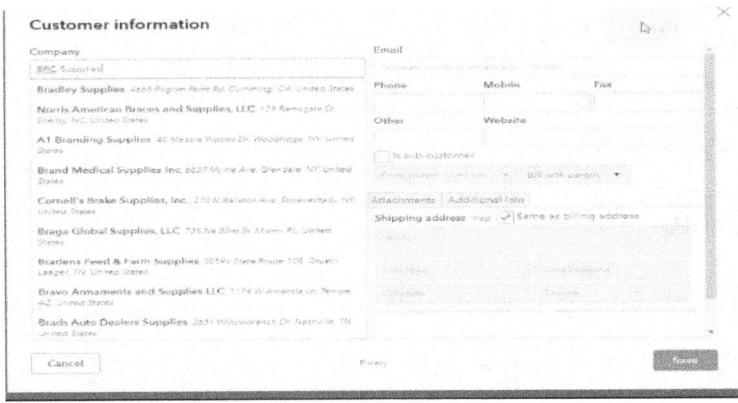

Upon entering a few characters, a list of potential matches and their addresses will appear, facilitating selection. However, since I'm entering this information manually, I will click elsewhere on the screen before completing the details.

Now, let us consider Tom Allen, the individual associated with this customer entry. Note that the display name defaults to Tom Allen. You can modify the display name to showcase either the company name or the last name, first name format (last name comma first name). Consistency is key, especially in ensuring easy customer retrieval using the last name, first name convention. Unchecking the box, I will input Tom Allen for checks' clarity.

Moving to the right, I can include additional details such as Tom's email (Tom at Yahoo), phone number, mobile, fax, and website. If Tom is a sub-customer, I can select the corresponding checkbox and identify the main customer.

The next step involves entering the billing address. For instance, Tom resides at 123 Billings Road, Bayshore, California, 94326, USA. Note that the shipping address mirrors the billing address by default. Adjustments can be made if your shipping information differs.

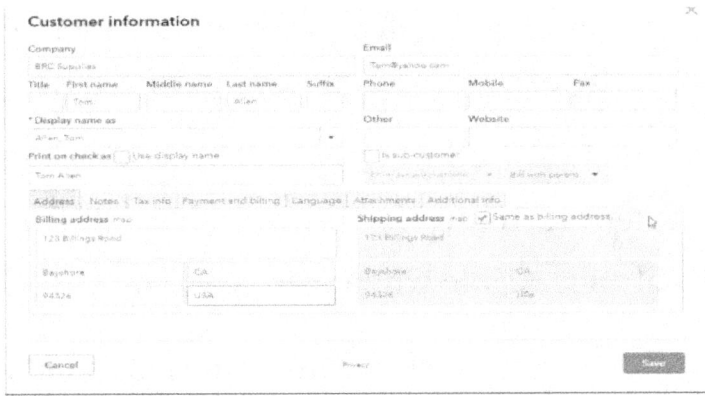

Clicking save, let's verify if Tom Allen is successfully added to the list. Here he is, under Allen, Tom.

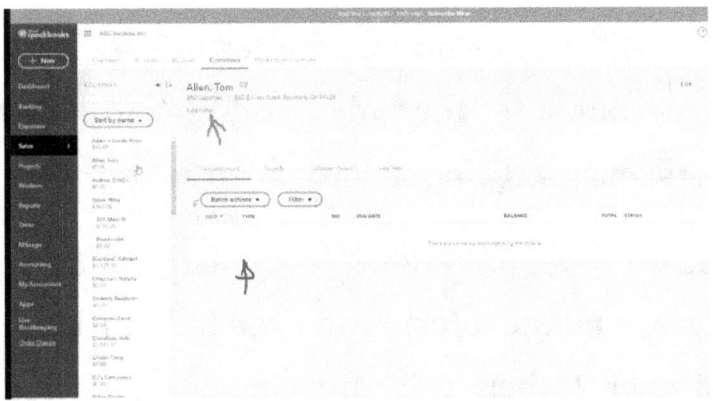

It's essential to highlight that once a customer is accidentally added, deletion is not an option. The online version of QuickBooks allows you to make a customer inactive, effectively hiding them from the list without permanent deletion.

Now, let's explore the information you have configured for Tom Allen. Take note of a couple of features: you have the option to add notes to this customer's record. Clicking on "Add Notes" (indicated with red arrow on the above picture), allows you to include details like "This is a new customer for the year 2024." This note will be easily accessible whenever needed.

Additionally, there is a tab for the transaction list below (Indicated with below arrow on the picture). Although there are no transactions at the moment, as we progress in creating invoices and receiving payments, these activities will be documented there. The "Projects" section pertains to the jobs undertaken for these customers; currently, none have been set up.

Moving on to "Customer Details," this section encompasses all the information you have just input for this customer. If there were any late fees, they would be visible when you click on the "late fees" as well. This essentially completes the process of setting up a new customer.

To go back to the list of customers, click on the "Customers" link at the top left. Notice that Tom Allen has an envelope icon to the right, indicating an email address has been provided for him. That is essentially how you add a new customer to your list.

Now, let's move to learning how to add a sub-customer. After mastering the process of adding a customer.

Adding Sub Customers

A sub-customer allows you to create a level beneath your main customer. This is useful when you have various jobs for a particular customer, and you want to separate them into sub-customers. This allows you to generate reports for the entire customer as well as per sub-customer. In the desktop version of QuickBooks, these are referred to as jobs or projects, but in this context, the term is a sub-customer. Let me guide you on setting these up.

To create a sub-customer, we will still use the new customer button since it's essentially a new customer being set up as a sub of an existing one. When the form appears, all you need to do is input the display name. In this example, they are using street addresses, so let's use "124 Scottsdale Drive." The only other thing you need to do is come to the "Is sub-customer" section and choose the parent customer you want to associate this sub-customer with (in this case I put Allen,Tom). You will notice it says "Bill with parent" on the right, and you should keep this together. Alternatively, you can bill this customer individually, but for now, let's leave it on "Bill with parent." You will see that it auto-fills information from Tom Allen's setup.

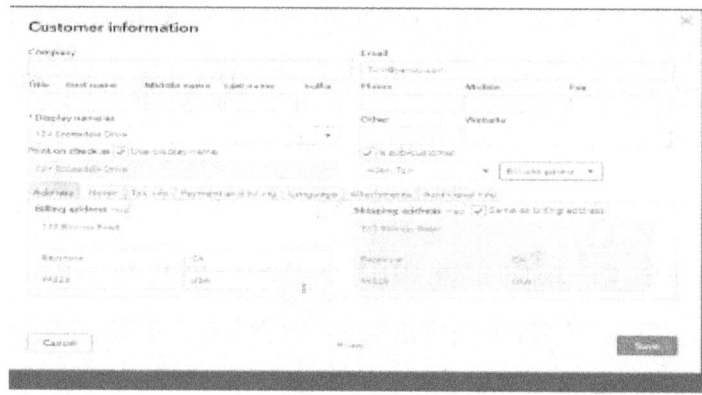

You do not need to change any of this unless it is different. Just hit save, and you have created your next level, visible right over here as you can see below;

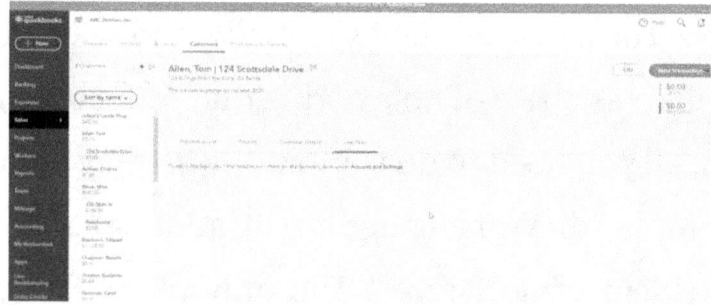

That is all there is to creating a sub-customer. Now, a couple of things you need to consider If you are utilizing the sub-customer feature, it is important to maintain consistency throughout QuickBooks. In case you do not, imagine you are working on a transaction, and instead of selecting 120 for Scottsdale, you accidentally choose Tom Allen. While it will still be allocated to the correct main customer, on reports, you will encounter 'Other,' prompting you to wonder, 'What's going on?' To avoid this, ensure you assign it to the appropriate sub-customer when utilizing the sub-customers option.

Not every business opts for the sub-customer feature, but it can be highly beneficial if you need to categorize various projects or have different locations for a specific customer. That sums up the essentials of working with sub-customers.

Editing Customers

Once you have set up a few customers, you may find the need to edit information. Whether it is an initial setup error or changes in customer details due to relocation, a new address, or the addition of a website, you can easily edit customer information. This demonstration below guides on how to do that:

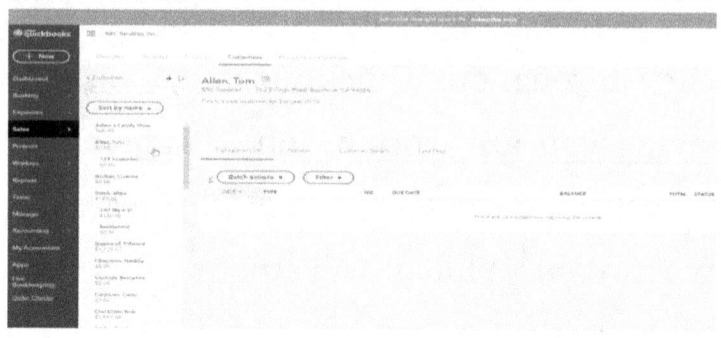

To edit a customer's details, click on the customer in the list (in this case Tom Allen), then choose the 'Edit' option. Let's consider an example – suppose Tom's email should include his last name. I will go ahead and add that. If, during the initial setup, you overlooked certain tabs, let's quickly go through them to understand the additional information you might want to configure for your customers.

We have covered the 'Address' tab; now, let's explore 'Notes.' This section allows you to add any relevant notes about the customer. Simply drop down after the previous note, input the date, and add any notes pertinent to that customer.

The third tab is 'Tax Info,' which pertains to collecting sales tax from the customer. If your business involves selling physical items with sales tax, inform QuickBooks about the customer's taxable status and the default tax code. While we will delve into sales tax details later, a heads up – when setting up the items or products and services you sell, you will establish each sales tax to collect. Later, you will group them for accurate customer charges, and that's where you'll input the tax code. For instance, if it's 'San Domingo,' select that.

Now, let's discuss what happens when we invoice a customer – it automatically pulls the tax code. Moving on to the next which is payment and billing. This section provides useful information for you. Firstly, the preferred payment method – does the customer usually pay with cash, check, barter, or MasterCard? You can find the list there. If you need to add a new payment method, like PayPal or Square, click 'Add New,' type the name, and save. PayPal is now on the list, indicating the customer's preferred method, though it doesn't mean they exclusively use it.

Consider the preferred delivery method: How do they want to receive their invoices? Print and later print them, or email for later reference? Or, do they have no preference?

Now, regarding terms, you can set different due dates for each customer. A loyal customer might have net 30 terms, while a new one might get a P.O.M. receipt. On the opening balance field – there, you specify the amount the customer owed you as of the start date of your company file. For instance, if it was $1,000, you could input that, ensuring correct accounting. However, some prefer not to fill this in, as long as the numbers reconcile. If you input an opening balance, include the date – usually the start date of your company file.

The 'Language' tab defaults to English, but if the customer prefers invoices in French, Spanish, or Italian, you can choose accordingly. The 'Attachments' option lets you add files related to the customer. Instead of searching your computer, open them directly in QuickBooks. The 'Additional Info' tab allows you to categorize customers based on your preferences – commercial, residential, or any custom classification.

After making changes, simply hit 'Save,' and the information is stored in QuickBooks. Regarding sales tax, be cautious – editing a customer's tax information won't alter previous invoices. It only applies to new ones created going forward. That wraps up editing customers.

<u>Making A Customer/customers Inactive</u>

In QuickBooks, for any list – customers, chart of accounts, vendors – you can make an item inactive temporarily, hiding it from the list. Inactive customers won't appear in other areas of QuickBooks, but you can reactivate them if needed. Let's see how to make a customer inactive.

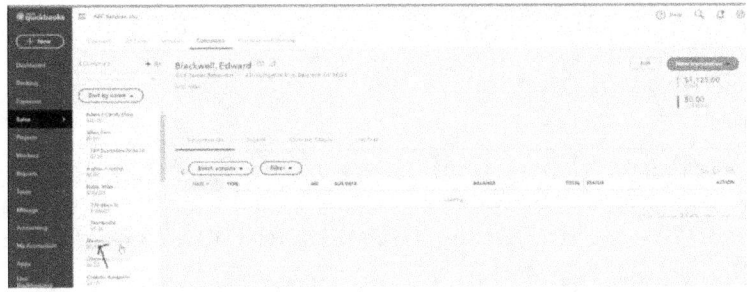

Suppose I want to make Edward Blackwell inactive, but he still owes $1,125. Generally, you can make a customer inactive if unused for a while. Let's explore what happens when attempting to make Mr. Blackwell inactive while he still owes money.

Click 'Edit.' And then below dialogue box come on your screen;

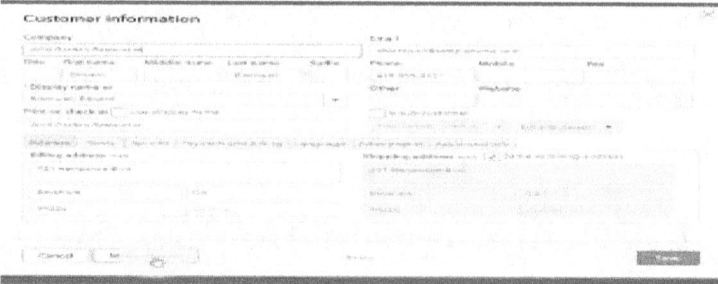

Then click "make inactive" The system warns that Edward has a balance. If you proceed, QuickBooks will create an adjusting entry to clear the debt. Confirming 'Yes' reveals an error due to a recurring template. To able to continue with this customer, you must first all delete that which is recurring. So, have to Cancel to try with another customer, say, Tom Allen, who has no outstanding balance.

Click on Tom Allen, and then click Edit on the right, make inactive. And now, it tells me that Tom has sub-customers or projects.

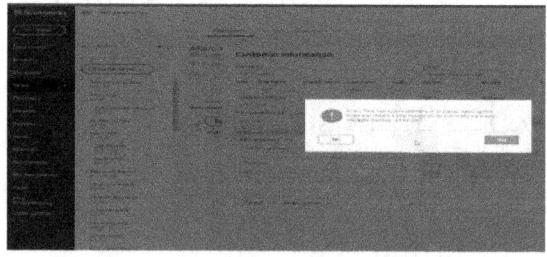

Making him inactive will also make all his sub-customers and projects inactive, and if that is what you want, click yes and now you will notice it says Tom Allen is deleted. Just a little FYI: QuickBooks does not have a feature to delete anything from a list, in this case, a customer. If you wanted to 'delete' them, you would have to make them inactive, and they are still not really deleted because they show up in the list; they are just hidden, so you can always activate them again. Now, if you notice over here;

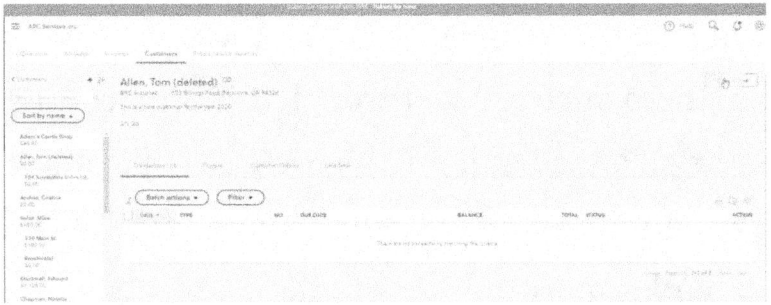

it says 'make active,' that is how If I want, go back and activate my customer again. I'm going to click make active, and now you will see over there on your chart, it does not say deleted, but notice the sub-customer does. You will repeat that process with your sub-customer: select them from the left and make them active. And that's a quick overview of how to make your customers inactive.

Importing Customers

To import your customers into QuickBooks; you might already have a list of your customers in Excel, for example, or in a CSV file, and it would be really nice to be able just to import them into QuickBooks instead of having to enter them one at a time. You will need to set them up a certain way. I want to go ahead and pull up the Excel file that I have so you can see how it's set up, and even if you don't have the fields the exact same, you can map them once you go through this import process. But let me go ahead and pull up the Excel file and show it to you and then pull up QuickBooks, and we will go through and import those customers.

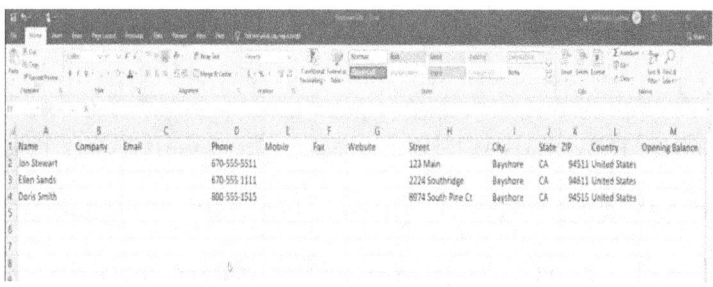

Here on the above picture on my excel, I have a list of three customers I would like to pull in from this Excel spreadsheet into QuickBooks, and you will notice that I have got them set up by name, company name, email, phone. You can see the list there; those are the names of the fields that are in QuickBooks that you want to pull the information into. If you can set it up this way, that is the best way to do it, but you can also map the fields if you want once you get inside QuickBooks. But I wanted you to see this so that you would know exactly how to set it up and make sure you save it somewhere that you can pull it in pretty easily when you go to look for it. Let me go ahead and flip over to QuickBooks, and we will pull in John, Ellen, and Doris. All you need to do is make sure you are in your customer list and go up to the down arrow next to 'New Customer' and choose 'Import Customers.'

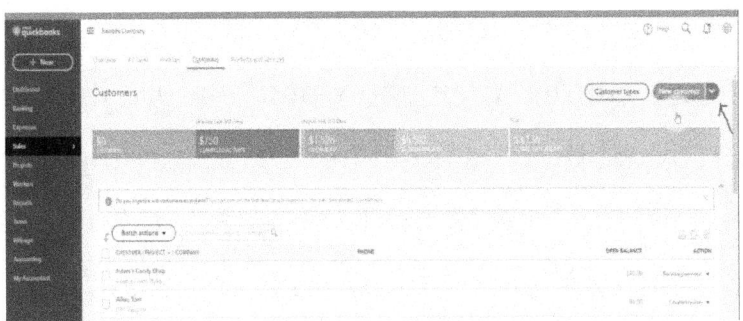

There is where you are going to select your Excel or your CSV file that you currently have your customers in by clicking on "browse"; mine's called 'customer list,' and I'll just choose that, and you can see it brought that file in. Now all I have to do is click 'Next' at the bottom, and here I can map my fields to the fields that are in QuickBooks.

You will notice the first column are the names of the QuickBooks fields, and the second column is the names of the fields you had in your file in excel. If the names do not match exactly, like this one says 'name,' but maybe in your Excel spreadsheet, this one said 'first name,' for example, then you would choose it from the down arrow. If there is not a match, like 'company,' for example, when I look in my Excel sheet, I did not have one 'company,' then I will just say 'no match,' and it won't be able to pull anything in. The ones with the checkmark that you see are the ones that actually have a match to the QuickBooks fields; it sees the exact same name that it sees over in your Excel spreadsheet. In this case, once you're finished going through that list, you can go ahead and click 'Next' at the bottom, and you will see that there are three customers now that are ready to be imported.

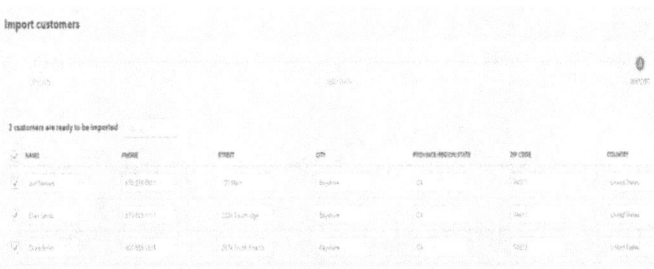

If I had a lot of these customers, I could go in and search for these by filtering and typing in the name of that customer; it is going to be pulling in the ones that have the checkmark next to them. To import all the three customers, click 'import' at the bottom.

On your customer list on QuickBooks chart of account, you will see that it has brought in those three customers. Let's look, first of all, for Mr. Stewart; we are going to go down the list, and you will notice that there is John Stewart;

he was the first one on our list; it has now imported all the information that was in that Excel spreadsheet.

Chapter six

Sales Overview

We have talked a lot about customers. Now that we have our customers in, we can now progress and talk about sales transactions using these customers. Here we are looking at all the different types of sales transactions that can occur when working with customers. These are going to be things like; you invoicing customers, are you receiving payments from those customers, maybe making deposits, credit memos, things like that. Before we get started, lets us go through very quickly the sales tab that is in QuickBooks and show you an overview of how it works and what type of information you can get out of it.

Once you are on QuickBooks, and we will look at the sales. Let's navigate to our navigation bar and point to sales, and then click on overview. This is just a quick overview of your income over time.

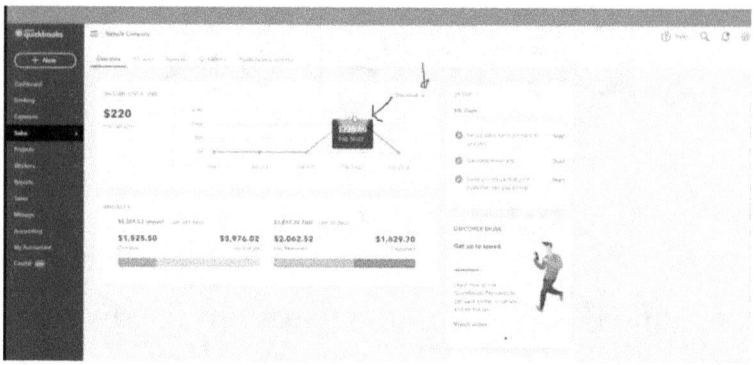

You can see that I have got two hundred and twenty dollars that it looks like I made this month, and I made that the week of February 16th through 22nd. Notice I can actually point right up there (I indicated with blue arrow) as well and see that information. If I wanted to change this and see how much I have made this month, this quarter, for example (click at the point indicated with red arrow on the picture above), you can see last year, this year, you have got different choices there. I'm going to go ahead and choose last month;

and it looks like last month we brought in over $7,000, and you can see the high points of when you brought in the most money. In this case, January 19 through 25 down there I can see how many invoices are overdue and also the ones that I already sent out that are not due yet, and that's three thousand nine hundred and seventy-six dollars. I might also have some money I have received that is not deposited yet, and you can see that there. Also, I can see the amount that I actually did deposit over on the right there.

Over there at the right, there are some things that you can opt to set up with QuickBooks, and some of these are paid subscriptions, but if you want to set these up, you have got different ways customers can pay you. That would be Apple pay if you want them to be able to pay you direct deposit, things like that. You can set those up with Intuit. You can also set up to get paid anywhere. So, if you have an app you have downloaded to your phone, you can accept payment right there or you can send out an invoice to your customer that they can pay online and they can actually click that invoice and then pay you right then and there. like I said some of these services are paid for, you will want to look into those before you sign up with one of those subscriptions. If you are interested in learning how the QuickBooks payments allow you to get paid online or in person you can watch this video there (where I indicated with red arrow on the picture below);

and then they have some shortcuts below that place. this is a quick overview of your accounts receivable.

Now notice the next tab after the overview tab is the "all sales".

There will show all of your sales. There you will see all the information on any sales transactions. You can see all the transactions listed at the bottom so you are going to see invoices, payments, credit memos. If you look down the list, there is a time charge, there is a sales receipt or refund. Any transaction that happened with your customer is going to be on this list. You are going to see all the information about the transaction, the balance, the total and all the way over on the right you can take an action related to that particular transaction. If you click the down arrow, you'll see several options—copying, deleting, or sending a reminder. Your choices are visible there. Moving on to the next tab at the top, you will find the 'Invoices.' These are invoices that haven't been paid yet. Detailed information about each invoice, such as the balance, total, and whether it is overdue or partially paid, is displayed. You have various actions available if you want to take any related to these invoices.

Following that is the 'Customer' tab, which we have delved into extensively. The last tab is labeled 'Products and Services.' There, you manage items you either buy or sell to your customers—physical items, inventory, or services. For each, you can explore numerous options available under that particular tab. This provides a brief overview of how to utilize the sales option. Now, let's go back and delve into the process of creating sales receipts for customers who wish to purchase and pay simultaneously.

How To Create Sales Receipt For Customers

When recording a sale to a customer, there are different approaches. One method is to create a 'sales receipt,' akin to a point-of-sale scenario. If a customer makes an immediate purchase and provides the payment, you can consolidate all details into a single transaction and provide them with a receipt. Another method, which we will discuss later as we progress, involves invoicing customers—sending an invoice and receiving payment afterward. For now, let's concentrate on sales receipts. Switching over to QuickBooks, I will guide you on how to enter a sales receipt.

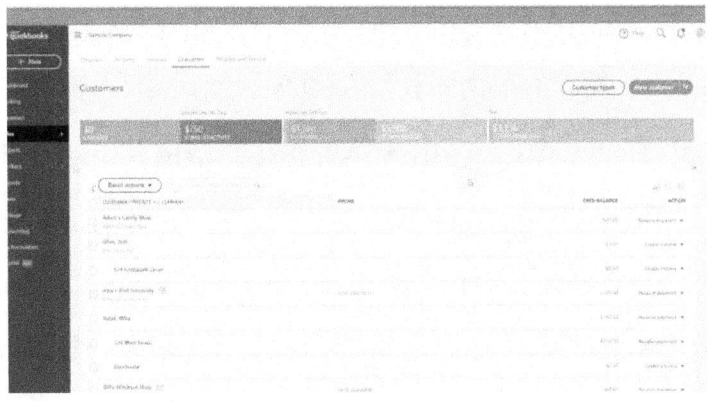

Begin by navigating to your customer list. Locate your customer and the sub-customer you want to send a sales receipt to. If you are using sub-customers, always choose the sub-customer. Selecting the main customer might lead to confusion in reports, as it will show as 'other,' without specifying what that refers to. When you click the down arrow on the far right, you will see the option to create a sales receipt.

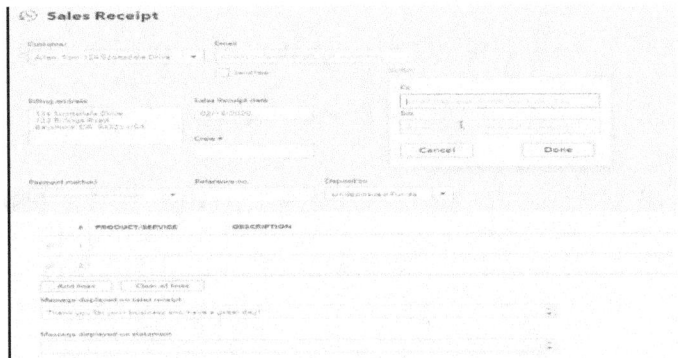

Initially, it imports the chosen customer and sub-customer. If needed, you can modify these by selecting from the drop-down list. Next, enter the email addresses if you intend to send this to more than one recipient. Separate multiple email addresses with a comma. If you need to CC or BCC additional email addresses, you will find those options there. There is also a checkbox labeled "send later." This is useful when you want to set up the sales receipt but delay sending it. Perhaps you are uncertain about the quantity, and you'd like to save the setup; you can do that.

In the billing address section, you will notice the sales receipt date, which is set to the current date. If you wish to change this date, simply click the small calendar icon, and select a new date. In this particular case, the sales receipt has a customized field labeled "crew number." You can input a number for the crew or leave it blank. We will revisit the payment method shortly; for now, let us move on to the product/service section.

Clicking in the first area reveals a drop-down list of all the products and services available for sale to your customer. For instance, there are garden rocks in the list. Upon selection, a description is populated, and you can edit or add to it. Enter the quantity and the rate;

let's assume these rocks are sold for $25 each. As you tab through, it will calculate the total. Note that physical items are usually subject to sales tax, unlike services. The trashcan icon at the end allows you to delete a line.

Now, let's add another item. Choose a service, such as a design service. Enter a description, set the quantity to 1, and establish the charge, say $100. Unlike the previous item, this service is not automatically subject to sales tax. You have a third line available; if it's not visible, click "add lines." You can also clear all the lines if needed.

Below, you'll find a message section that will be displayed on the sales receipt, currently saying "thank you for your business and have a great day." Feel free to personalize it. If you want a message to appear on statements, you can input it there where it says "message displayed on statement". On the right;

you will see the subtotal, with $75 subject to sales tax in this case. The sales tax is labeled California, set at 8%, resulting in $6. If you wish to offer a discount, you can specify a percentage or a value. For example, entering 10% deducts 18 cents

As I scroll down, it will display the amount received and the balance due. Now, remember, because this is a sales receipt, we are accounting for the payment amount, assuming we have received all of it. Up there where it says "payment method" is where I can choose the payment method. Whether paid with Visa or by check, I can select any option I prefer, with a dedicated space for a reference number. For Visa transactions, no reference number is needed; however, for a check, it would be the check number.

The next item you will encounter after the reference no tab is "deposit to -" indicating "undeposited funds."

Alternatively, you could choose to deposit it directly into a checking account, for example. The options are visible in the list. Briefly "undeposited funds." In your chart of accounts, you will find an account named "undeposited funds." It serves as a temporary holding place for collected money that has not yet been deposited into the bank. If a customer pays you with a check and you want to acknowledge the sale as paid, you would opt for "deposit to undeposited funds." However, if you plan to consolidate all today's receipts into one large deposit, you would choose "undeposited funds." If you knew this deposit only contained the current transaction, you could opt for "checking" and bypass the subsequent deposit step. I'll leave it in "undeposited funds," and when you are done, at the bottom, you can either save or choose "save and send" to email it. Alternatively, from the drop-down arrow, you can select "save and close." We'll close this, completing the transaction.

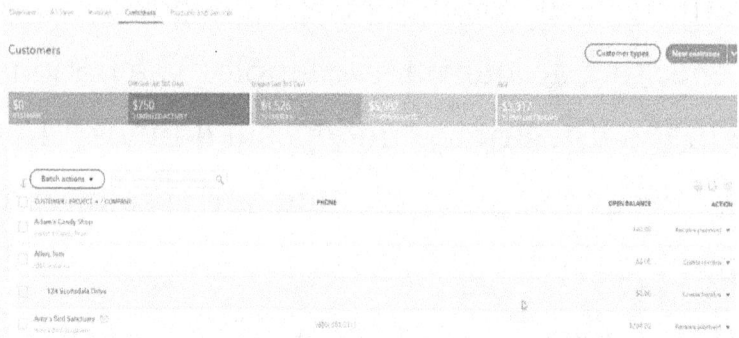

Upon inspection, you will notice that Tom Allen at 124 Scottsdale doesn't owe us any money. However, if we go to "all sales" and look, we should find Tom Allen's sales receipt right there, amounting to $180.82, marked as paid. There under the "Action column" is where we could go to print the receipt or click the drop down and any other actions I wish. If I wish to view or edit the sales receipt, you choose that from the drop-down option and you will see that this is your sales receipt, allowing you to make changes if needed. I will exit this by hitting the X and canceling it. This demonstrates how to create a sales receipt, with the funds now residing in "undeposited funds."

Now, navigate to your chart of accounts, found under "accounting," to view the funds. In the chart of accounts, you will find "undeposited funds." It currently holds $2,243. Viewing the register there will display the recent transaction, alongside any others previously in "undeposited funds." Keep this in mind as we discuss making deposits later. Monitoring "undeposited funds" is a way to ensure everything has been deposited, as there shouldn't be any remaining balance

Alright, let's explore the process of invoicing customers. We have touched upon sales receipts, and now it's time to delve into the world of sending invoices to your customers. The fundamental difference between a sales receipt and an invoice lies in the context. With a sales receipt, the customer is physically present; you input the purchased items and record the payment right there. On the other hand, an invoice is where you dispatch a billing document to your customer, anticipating payment at a later date. Whether you transmit these invoices via email or traditional mail is inconsequential; the key is that you'll be collecting the payment down the line.

Chapter seven

Invoicing Customers

Here we are going to go through the steps of crafting invoices for your customers. The process is akin to creating sales receipts, but I' show you where to initiate the invoice creation. There are a couple of routes to commence crafting an invoice. Navigate to the navigation pane and hover over "sales." From there, you can either opt for the "invoice" feature or explore the "customers" option.

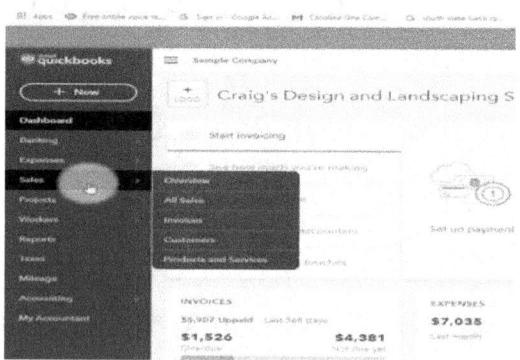

If you opt for the "invoices" section, you will encounter a list of your current invoices. To generate a new one, simply select "new invoice" from this menu (where is written new invoice). If you initiated the process from the "customers" section, return to "sales" and proceed to "customers.

If you had a customer that need to create invoice for, check the box of the customer on your customer list and move to the right and click on the drop-down arrow on the action column and select create invoice and it will take you there;

Notice, because you a selected customer to invoice, QuickBooks pulled in all the customers information and if you wish to change the customer, click on the drop-down arrow under customer on the invoice plan and choose another customer, always remember to pick sub-customer if you are using sub-customer so that you do not see "other" when you look report.

If you did not have your customer email type in your customer set, you can physically input the customer email under "customer email"

From the invoice plane, you can do lots things like CC or BCC someone by clicking on the tab associated to the task you want to initiate. If you Check the box for "send later" it actually means you can create this invoice, you want to just fill this invoice and save it, then create another invoice and check the same box. If you actually did, you can email both of them at same time; this is called sending batch or emailing in batch.

If it happens that something has change with the customers billing address, you effect the changes under the "billing address" there. Doing this will prompt you when you want to save it if you want to save the changes permanently on the customers' record.

Under term is where you set when you want the invoice to be due to you, it is the number of days from invoice date to due date. If you set the term to Net 30, it actually means you want the invoice to be due to you in 30 days.

On the product/service tab, you pick the product or service you want to invoice this customer for. In this case I will pick installation of landscape design, then you will fill the quantity and rate at which you charge the customer. Since service is nontaxable, the box under tax will be unchecked but if it happens to be checked when invoicing for service, just uncheck it. On where it is written "message on invoice" is where you type that message that will appear on your invoice automatically. The same goes for where you have "message on statement", there is where you type message that appears on statement if you are sending statement to your customer.

When you scroll down, you will notice that you can also attach a file under attachment tab. To illustrate, if you have a file saved on your computer, you can attach it there. For instance, if I'm working on a landscape design project and I have hired a subcontractor, they might have already sent me a bill that I want to attach to this invoice.

On the right side, if you plan to offer your customer a discount, you can provide either a percentage discount or a value discount. Click on the drop-down arrow on the "discount value tab". There I will choose a value and give them $25, and you will see it deducted from the total of $200. So, the balance due is now $175. At the bottom, you have a few options: you can print or preview the invoice right there. You can also set it as recurring, meaning if this is a regular occurrence, QuickBooks can automatically insert this invoice at the specified intervals. For instance, once a month, it can insert this invoice automatically, and you can further customize it, perhaps adding fields like a crew number.

Down the bottom at your right, you have options like "save," "save and close," and if you wish to create a new invoice, you could click the arrow and choose "save and new." However, I'll opt for "save and close," and now our invoice is completed. If I want to review it later, I can go to "invoices," look through the list, and find the specific one I'm looking for.

Recording Customer Payments

Here, I will be guiding you on recording a payment once a customer pays you. After you have created your first invoice, the customer will send you a payment. It doesn't matter how they pay; you will record their payment in the same way. We will inform QuickBooks about the payment amount, date, and other relevant information. Once done, the invoice will reflect as paid, showing the full amount paid, any remaining balance, or an overpayment. Let me walk you through the process of recording a customer payment.

Before we receive the first payment, let's head over to the report section in QuickBooks. Simply navigate to your navigation bar, click on "reports," and then choose "reports" from the menu as shown below.

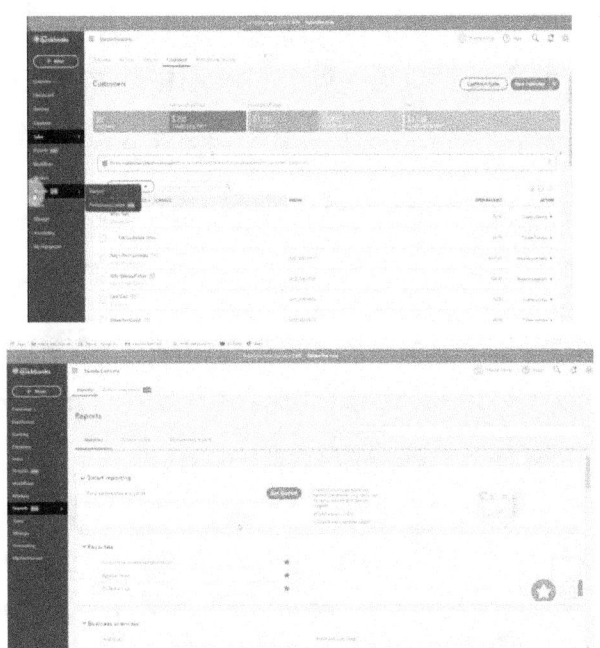

These are all the reports available in QuickBooks (refer to the second picture). While we will explore these reports later, for now, let's scroll down and go to the "who owes you" section, specifically the "open invoices report" in the second column. Click to run that report. Those are all the invoices you have sent out that haven't been paid yet. Even if the customer owes you a small amount, as seen in the previous section where in this case I created an invoice for Freeman Sporting Goods and one for 25 Twin Lake, I can click on the link in any report to access that specific transaction

I wanted to highlight this first because once we payment is received, this invoice will either disappear if it's paid in full, or you will see the invoice and the balance owed, not the original $175 it was invoiced for. Now that you've observed that, let's return to our customers. Navigate to sales and then customers. Now, locate the customer for whom we are receiving payment; in this case, it is Freeman Sporting Goods, 55 Twin Lake. Refer to the picture below

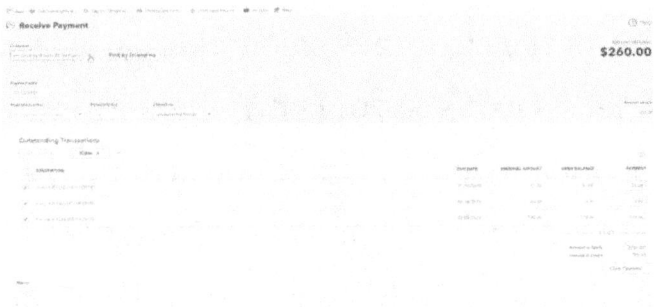

In the action column, you will notice the option to "Receive Payment." This opens the payment window.

Initially, it auto-filled with the customer and job details, which you generally don't need to change unless you are selecting a different customer or job. If you are searching for an invoice by number, you can simply click there on "find invoice by number", type in the invoice number, and hit find. Moving on, specify the payment date; for instance, let's say it was received on February 28th. Now, select the payment method. There, you can choose how the customer paid you—

cash, MasterCard, Visa, PayPal, or any other methods you'd like to add (such as Venmo, Square, or Bitcoin) by clicking "Add New. "For this example, let's assume it was a check. Enter the check number in the reference number field. Note that the money will be directed to an account named undeposited funds.

On the right side, QuickBooks assumes the customer paid the entire outstanding balance for all their invoices, which may not always be the case. Input the actual amount the customer paid (where it says amount received); let's say it's $179. Down the bottom, you will see a list of open invoices. QuickBooks often distributes the payment across all invoices; however, you can adjust this if needed. For instance, if the customer is not paying the first one, they might be allocating $175 to the last one and $4 to another. Ensure you have the correct invoices checked and the accurate amounts applied.

Observing the bottom, you will find $179 worth of money applied, and currently, there are no credit memos. If you issued one for this customer, you could apply it there to one of those invoices of that customer that is opened there. To clear the payment, you have that option as well, enabling you to start over with the form. There's also a memo section on the left and a space for attachments if needed.

This covers the process of receiving payments, which is quite straightforward. Now, let's revisit the "undeposited funds" aspect under the "deposit to" option and discuss your current options.

If you receive payments, they are directed to an account known as undeposited funds. Let me quickly save this, and then I'll guide you to where undeposited funds is.

Now, if I close the "Receive Payment" window and navigate back to the chart of accounts, I'll go to Accounting > Chart of Accounts. In the list, you will spot an account named undeposited funds, currently holding in this case $2,241.52. This serves as a temporary holding place for money received but not yet deposited into the bank. To ensure accuracy, if everything's been deposited, this should read zero.

Take a moment to examine this. Click to view the register on the right, and you will observe three payments currently residing in undeposited funds, including the recent one. None of these payments have made it to the checkbook as they await deposit.

Now, let's return to the payment we recently discussed. I will go to Sales, back to Customers, and locate our customer Freeman Sporting Goods at 55 Twin Lake. I will click on that for a moment, and you will find the payment we just received. Clicking on it reopens the details.

Consider your options there. You could directly deposit the money into the checking account, bypassing the next step. However, let me explain why you may or may not want to choose this. If the $179 is the sole amount in that deposit, select "Checking," hit "Save and Close" at the bottom, and you are done with the process. But if you anticipate receiving another payment, possibly from a different customer, and plan to deposit this and the new payment together, that's when you should opt for undeposited funds. This will become clearer when we proceed to make the deposit, click "Save and Close" at the bottom now, and let's confirm if the invoice indicates it's been paid. Looking at the $175 invoice, it does show as paid in full. If there was even a penny left, it wouldn't display "paid" right there. That's the procedure for receiving a payment for a customer after sending out an invoice. The subsequent step in the process is to take that money and make a deposit.

How To Make Deposit In QuickBooks

Having successfully completed a sale and invoiced a customer, we have received payment, and now our goal is to deposit that money into the bank. Enter the "Make Deposits" option—an integral step always concluding this process, irrespective of the payment method, be it Visa card, cash, or cheque. Ensuring that your QuickBooks deposits align with actual bank transactions is paramount.

Now, let's transition to QuickBooks and explore the "Make Deposits" option.

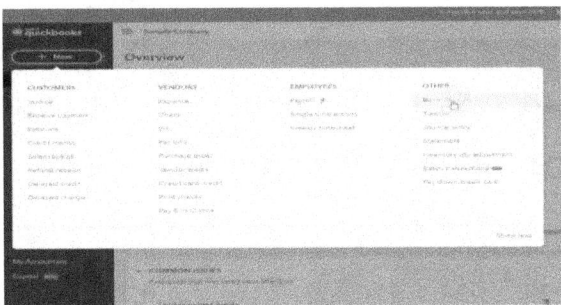

To record the deposit seamlessly, click the "New" button, and under "Other," locate "Bank Deposit."

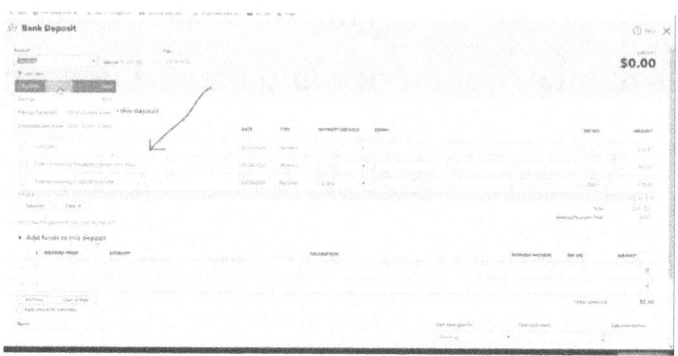

This window represents your actual deposit slip. It is crucial to double-check that you have selected the correct bank account, preventing any confusion that may arise if the last-used account automatically populates the field.

Observe that the account in this case is "checking account" and the balance is $1,201, and the designated deposit date is March 2nd. Now, down at the bottom, there are the three sets of monies that we saw sitting in undeposited funds (indicated with red arrow on the above picture). What you are going to do is check off all of the ones that are going in this deposit. If all three are going to be in this deposit, you check them all off. If maybe the first two are going to be in that deposit and then maybe the last one was in a separate deposit, do them separately because you want these to match what actually happened at the bank. Let's say, in this case, though, all three are going to be deposited.

A couple of things when you are looking at this list there: you can go and change the payment type if you didn't do it when you were actually receiving the payment. You have also got a place for a memo; you can fill that if you like. And then you can see there is the reference number column and then the amount column over on the right. My deposit will be $2,241.52. Now, right down as you go, it says "Cashback goes to." If you happen to have a business bank account, you are not going to be able to get cash back. But as a sole proprietor, you could. If you are going to keep some cash, then you would say "Cashback goes to this account," and you would pick whichever account this went to. You would also be able to have a memo, and if you were going to keep 20 bucks, you could type that in under "cash back amount", and it would deduct it from this total right up there.

There is also a place to add funds to this deposit. If I click this little arrow there, it is going to open up this part below it, and I can add some additional monies. Now, this could be something like maybe you got a rebate from Staples. You could type that in. If that was the situation, it would say "Received from Staples," the account would be "Office Expenses" or "Office Supplies." Pick whichever account you actually use when you purchased the items for that rebate and put it back to the same account

maintaining accurate records of your financial transactions

In your transaction record, there are distinct sections for a description, the method used, and the amount of money involved. If you are planning to contribute personal funds to the business, designate the account as owner equity. Although we covered this concept previously, it is crucial to remember that not every deposit represents income for the business. Therefore, ensure that additional funds are correctly allocated to the appropriate account.

If you require more than the allotted two lines, feel free to add extra lines as needed by clicking on "add lines" at the bottom. You also have the option to include a memo with the deposit or attach relevant documents at the bottom. Following these steps will complete the deposit process.

Beyond these essential steps, there are additional features you may explore. For instance, you can print the deposit details or set it up as a recurring transaction by clicking on "print or make recurring button" at the bottom. Consider scenarios where a customer is on automatic draft, regularly paying, let's say, $1,000 monthly—this would be reflected in the deposit. The possibilities are diverse.

Upon completion, click "Save and Close" at the bottom. At this point, the deposited amount, in this case, $2,241.52, will be reflected in your checking account.

With this, the entire sequence—from invoicing a customer to receiving payment and making the deposit—has been successfully executed. Now, let's navigate to the checking account (refer to the picture below) to locate and verify the transaction.

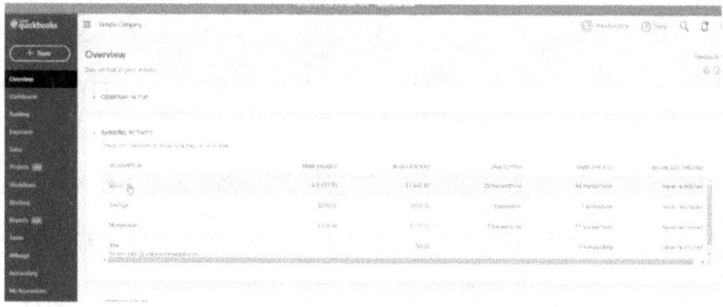

Currently, on the overview section there, right where we are on the above picture, you fill find the checking account. This provides a convenient link for checking the balance. Alternatively, you can navigate to the accounting section, access the chart of accounts, and open it from there. Either method is effective. For now, let's proceed to view the register. Within the register, you will notice my recent deposit. It is labeled as "split" because it involves multiple line items. In this instance, three different transactions contributed to the deposit. I will cancel this for now, concluding the process of making a deposit.

Setting Up Credit Memos For Customers

There are instances when issuing a credit memo for an invoice becomes necessary. For example, if a customer expresses dissatisfaction with your services and refuses payment for an invoice, you may choose to credit it off after some time. Allow me to demonstrate how to create a credit memo.

Begin by looking up the original invoice you have created to identify the charged items.

For instance, for Red Rock Diner, there's an invoice for $70 related to pest control (when you click on that particular invoice to open it up), comprising probably two hours at $35 per hour.

Now, assuming the customer is dissatisfied, and we want to credit that invoice, we need to use the exact same product or service initially charged.

To create the credit memo, click on "New" on the navigation bar and under customers and select "Credit Memo." Enter the customer's name, such as Red Rock Diner, and you will see it auto-populate their email, billing address, with the current date for the credit memo. Ensure you enter the desired date for the credit memo

Specifically, we will input "pest control" there, emphasizing the importance of crediting the same product or service initially invoiced. Opting for a quantity of two at $35 each, we arrive at a total of $70. Simply proceed to "Save and Close."

Now that the credit memo is generated, I will highlight two changes on your customer's account. Observe the closed credit memo and the appearance of a new payment. To correctly apply the $70 to the outstanding invoice, click on the payment. If it identifies an exact match, it will automatically check it off; otherwise, manually select the appropriate invoice. Ensure both the invoice and credit memo are checked at the bottom. The amount to apply is $70, and you can finalize the process by clicking "Save and Close" at the bottom.

Given the interconnected nature of this transaction, you will be prompted to confirm the modification. Proceed with a "yes." Upon reviewing, you will find the credit memo and payment closed, and the invoice marked as paid. Remember, this is a two-step process— first, create the credit memo, then return to the payment to apply it to the correct invoice.

Refunds: How To Issue Refund To Customers.

There are instances when a refund is warranted, such as when a customer has paid in full for a purchase, and you intend to return their money. Unlike credits, which typically sit in their account until deducted, refunds involve giving customers their money back. I'll guide you through creating a refund receipt, but first, let's look up the customer to determine the specifics of the refund.

For example, Duke's Basketball Camp has a fully paid invoice for $460.40. Opening the invoice reveals they purchased six garden rocks at $12 each, and now they wish to return three. With this information, we can proceed to create the refund receipt

Now, let's click a new option in the navigation and select refund receipts under customers column. First, select the customer's name; in our case, it's Duke's Basketball Camp. The system will automatically populate their email and billing address. Ensure the correct refund receipt date is entered. Under "Payment Method," specify how the customer originally paid; for instance, if they paid by check, and you're refunding from your checking account, you can decide whether to print a check later or input the check number now.

Next, choose the appropriate product or service—in this instance, garden rocks. They are returning three at $12 each, totaling $36. If the original purchase included sales tax, QuickBooks will automatically account for the tax refund. The total refunded amount will be $38.88. Click "Save and New" to complete the refund receipt. Upon a successful transaction, click OK.

Returning to the customer's account, you will now see the paid refund. If you wish to print a check, click "Print

Check" on the right. Confirm that the correct checking account is selected at the top and verify the check number. If it is a cash refund, choose the cash option in the refund receipt.

At this point, you can preview and print the refund receipt. Simply click on "Preview," then proceed to print. That concludes the process of creating a refund for a customer, known as a refund receipt.

How To Give Credit To A Customer

You can use QuickBooks Online to issue credits to your customers. You might want to do this to reduce what a customer owes on an invoice or to write off the balance of an invoice you'll never receive like bad debt. Credits are different from refunds. You issue a refund when you send moneyback to a customer, you issue a credit to reduce what a customer owes you now or in the future. If you want to record a refund.

We'll go over how to record a credit memo, send it to a customer, and then apply it to an invoice.

To start, on the navigation pane Select new Credit Memo.

Note that it's important not to go back and edit invoices that you've already sent. If you change an invoice after you've sent it, you risk changing information from a prior period. To change the customer's balance the right way, use a credit memo;

Select the customer you want to give a credit to.

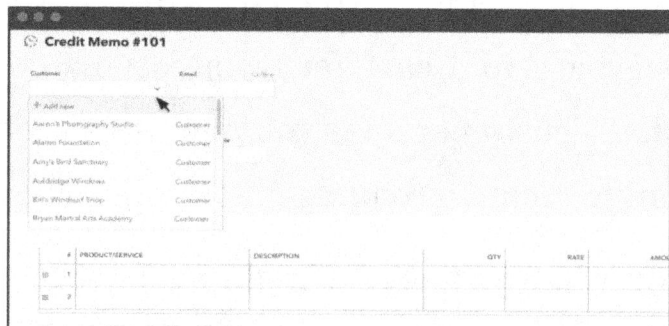

Then select the products and services you want to give them credit for;

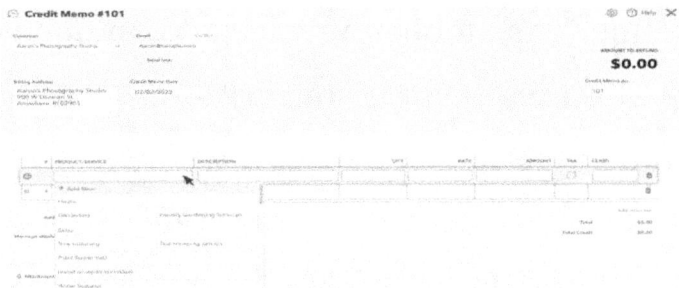

If this is a credit related to a specific invoice, you should usually use the same products and services you used on the invoice. Then add the amount of the credit you want to give them. If you want to send a copy of the credit memo to your customer, select, save and send at the bottom. Otherwise. Select, Save and Close.

Now let's go over how to apply the credit memo. Navigate back to your customers window and click on the customer you want to issue credit to and open the customer's record to see how each step affects the customer's balance and open transactions.

This customer has an open invoice and an open credit memo (written unapplied) you just issued to them. If your customer has an open invoice with you, you could wait until they pay you to apply the credit memo. But if you want to apply the credit memo immediately, head to the navigation pane, select new, under customers, select receive payment;

Then enter the customer's name;

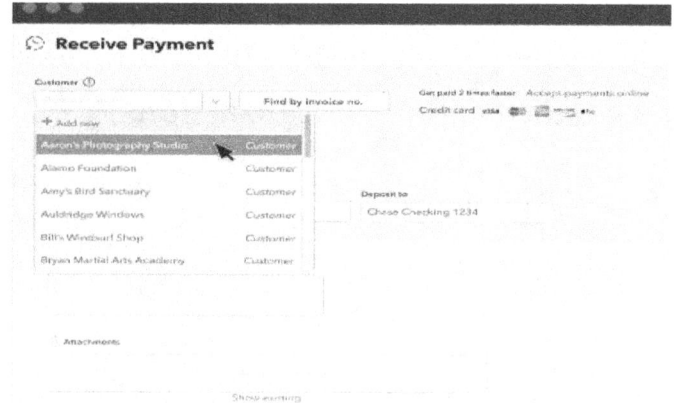

QuickBooks automatically selects the credit memo and the oldest open invoice.

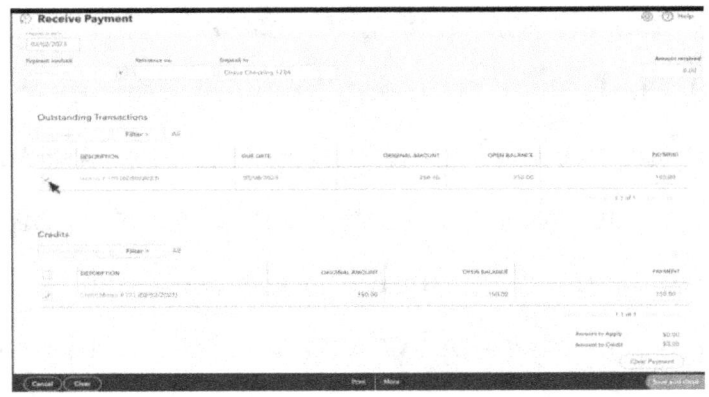

If this is the invoice, you want to apply the credit memo to select, Save and Close. If you want to apply the credit memo to a different invoice, the steps are different. You need to go back to the navigation plane, click on new, under customer select receive payment and select or search for the customer to apply the credit to; Note that because this is a complicated subject, it's important to follow directions very closely to avoid mistakes. Unselect the credit memos (it is important to perform this step first), unselect the invoice then select the invoice you want to apply the credit to, select the credit you want to apply, and then change the amount received to zero. If you only want to apply part of the credit to the invoice, change the payment amount. This should leave you with a $0 payment that applies the credit memo to the invoice. Select, Save and Close. QuickBooks closes the credit memo and marks the invoices closed or partially closed. If there's a remaining balance. If you don't usually have more than one open invoice with your customers, or it just doesn't matter to you which invoice QuickBooks apply is a credit to, you can change your settings so that QuickBooks always applies credits to the oldest open invoice.

To affect these settings, Select Settings (by clicking on the gear icon) and under your company, select "Account and Settings".

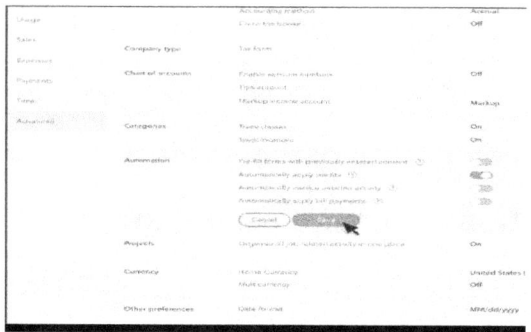

Then select Advanced and select automation, then turn on automatically apply credits and save. Note that you can still change which invoice gets the credit if you need to. By following the steps we went over before.

Now you're ready to record and apply credit memos to adjust your customers balances.

How To Create Estimates

An estimate allows you to give your customer quote or proposal for work you plan to do. We will be dealing on how to create an estimate in QuickBooks Online, some of your customization options, and how to email it to your customer for review. Then we'll show you where to check on the status of your estimate. To start a new estimate, select New and then under the customer column, select "Estimate".

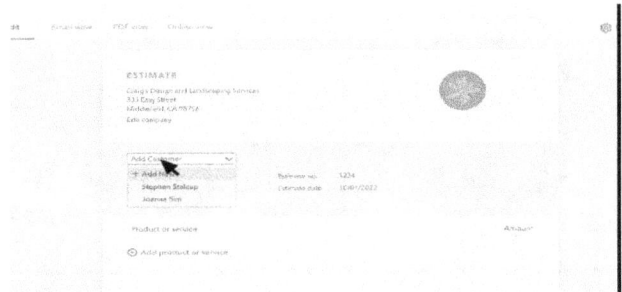

If you don't see them, you can add them by selecting the add new customer tab there. You'll see your customer's address and email if you've already added them to QuickBooks. If not, fill them in and hit save and close.

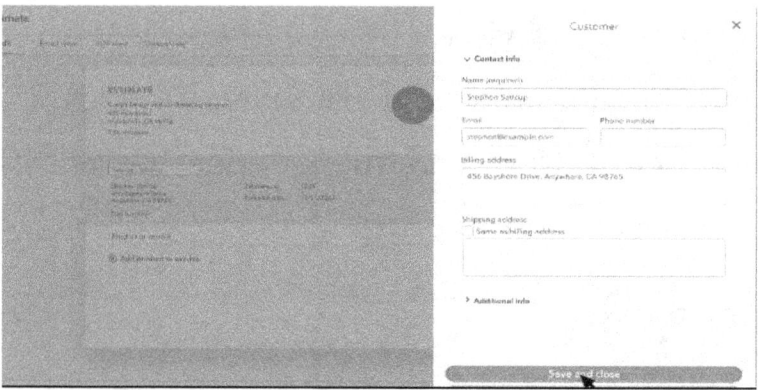

Next, select Add product or service and enter your proposal for this estimate. If you need to add a new product or service, you can do that there.

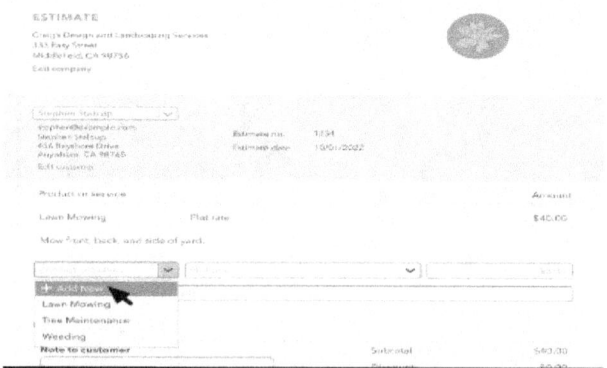

Add or adjust the quantity and rate as needed for this estimate. You can also add any notes you want displayed on the estimate or attach photos that provide more information about the project.

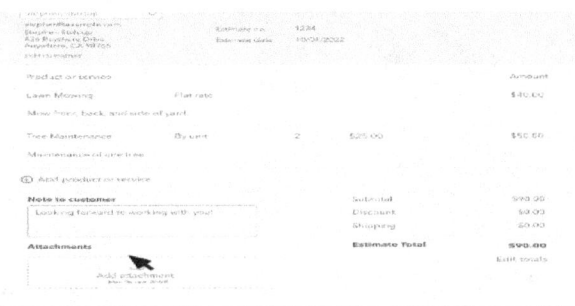

When you're finished, select email.

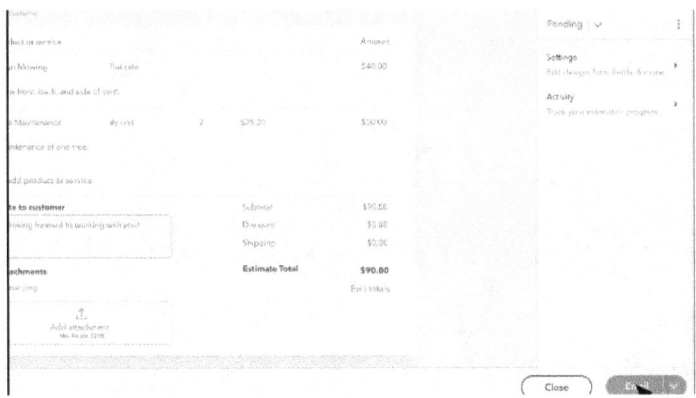

You'll see the email your customer will receive, which includes a link where they can review and approve your estimate online. When you're ready, select Send estimate.

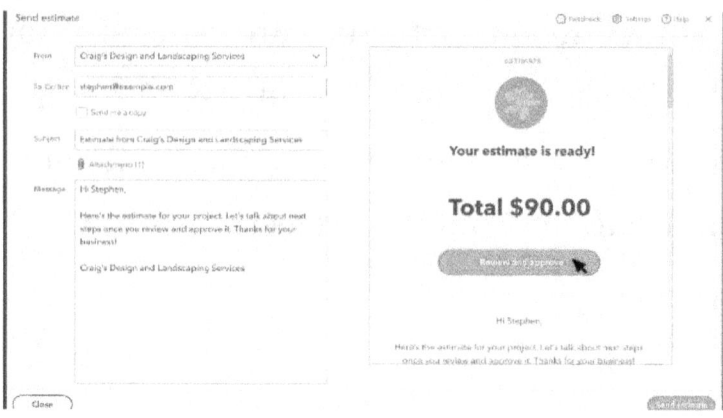

In the estimates list, you can see the status of your estimate, including when your customer has viewed it.

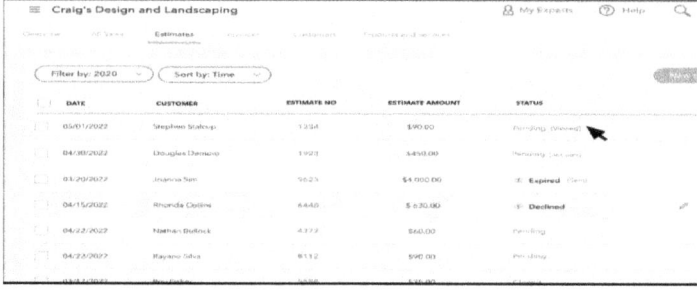

Note Your navigation may look like picture below.

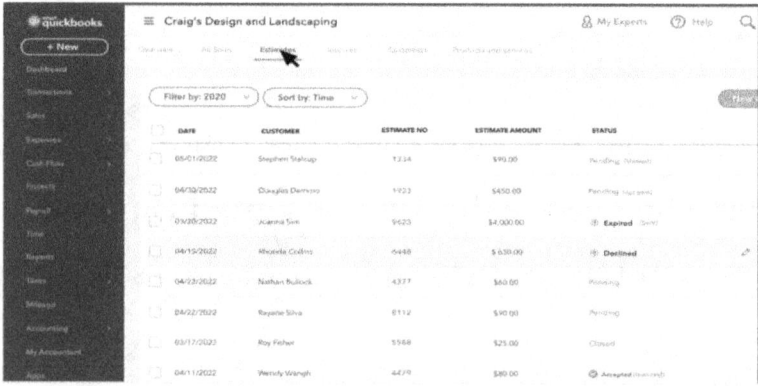

And, you can also create estimates on the go with the QuickBooks Mobile app. This concludes the process.

How To Convert An Estimate To An Invoice

Once your customer accepts your estimate, the next step is to convert that estimate into an invoice so you can bill them. Let's go over how to track an estimate's status and how to convert an estimate to an invoice in QuickBooks Online. To view an estimate's status, first select Estimates. Note your navigation may look like this.

When you send the estimate to your customer through QuickBooks, you'll be able to see when your customer has viewed, accepted, or declined the estimate.

When a customer has accepted your estimate online, the status will be accepted. Or if you received word of mouth commitment, then you can manually mark your estimate as accepted.

To create an invoice from an estimate. Select convert to invoice next to the relevant estimate. You can also select the estimate, select more actions, and convert to invoice.

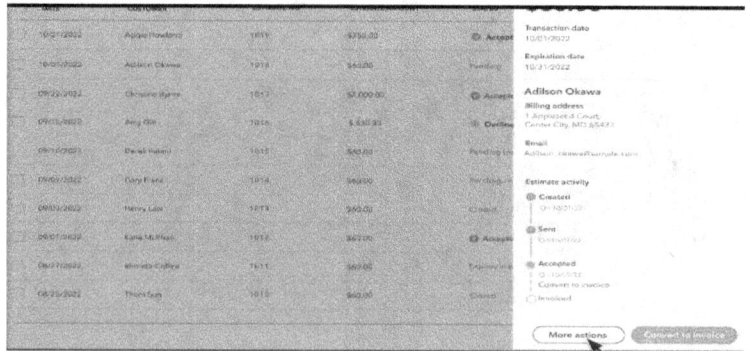

QuickBooks will automatically fill in the invoice based on the estimate, including products or services used. If you need to change any of the quantities or rates, or even add more products and services on this invoice, you can do that. You will be able to preview your invoice in different forms, including seeing what a PDF, email and payment view looks like. Once you're satisfied, select email.

When you send an invoice via QuickBooks, you get better visibility of its status, including when a customer viewed it through the invoice list. That's it. Now you can easily keep track of your estimates and seamlessly create and send invoices to get paid once you've completed the work.

How To Pay Sales Tax

When you set up your sales tax, QuickBooks automatically keeps track of what you owe and when so you can avoid late returns and penalties. Before we progress let us touch on where you can find out how much tax you need to pay to which agencies and when. Then, once you pay your taxes, how to record that payment in QuickBooks. Note that you cannot pay your taxes from QuickBooks Online. You'll have to pay at your tax agency's website or send in a payment by mail. To start, go to the sales tax center.

You'll see any taxes you owe for the on the above picture range. If your taxes are overdue you might need to change the(due date start and due date end) range to find them. As long as you entered in the correct sales tax settings and your books are accurate then your tax amounts will be accurate.

If you need to adjust your sales tax settings you can do that there. Select 'View return' and you'll see exactly how much you owe in state, county and local taxes if relevant.

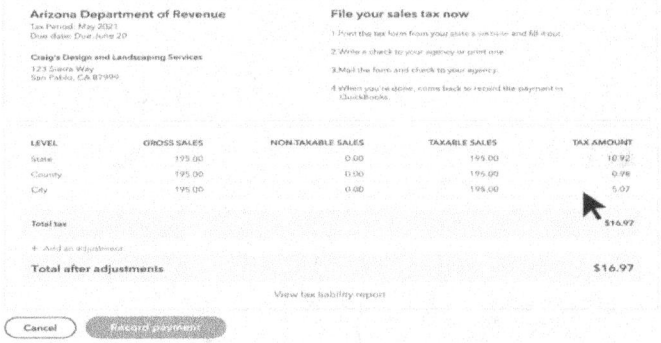

If you want a more detailed look at what you owe for this period select "View tax liability report" at bottom.

This is helpful if you want to review your taxable and non-taxable invoices, receipts, and other transactions. The total (I indicated with a red arrow in the above picture) tells you how much you owe in taxes based on your taxable income for that period. However, if the amount you need to pay is different because of credits, discounts, penalties or a correction, then you can add an adjustment.

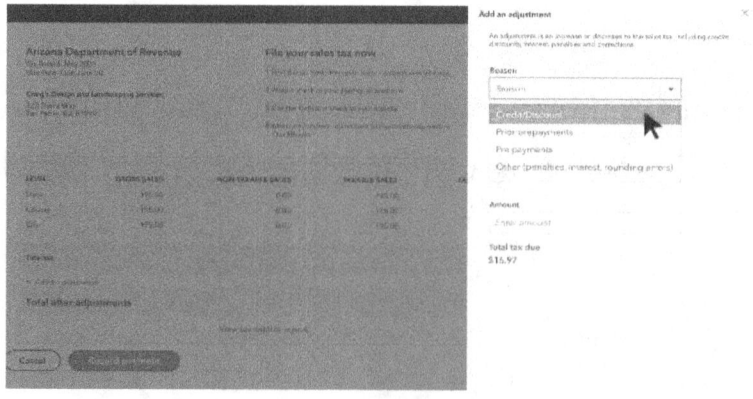

Enter in the reason for the adjustment and the date. Then select the account. If you owe more money then you'll select an expense account. If you owe less, then you'll select an income account.

In this example we are getting a discount for paying early. Enter in the amount of the adjustment then select Add. Then you'll see that QuickBooks adds your adjustment and gives you a new total. Now you are ready to pay your taxes. Most states encourage businesses to e-file. But if you can't file online, you can check your tax agency's website for more info on how to mail your return. Go to your tax agency's website to file your return online. Fill out your sales tax return form. Once you are finished paying your taxes go back to QuickBooks and record the payment.

Enter the payment date and the bank account you used to pay your taxes. When you are done select Record payment. Now you have paid your sales taxes and recorded them in QuickBooks to keep your books accurate.

How To Create Statements For Your Customers

Sending statements is a helpful feature that serves as a gentle reminder to customers about their outstanding balances. Typically sent at the end of each month, these statements detail the activity throughout that period. While not mandatory, it's a useful tool to keep customers informed about their account status.

To create statements, navigate to QuickBooks navigation pane and click on the new option and under the "Other" option click on "Statement" in the dropdown menu. The first step is selecting a statement type; options include balance forward, any open items for the last year, and transaction statement. Let us choose "Balance Forward." Specify the statement date, usually at the end of the month, with the start date as January 1 and the end date as January 31. For customer balance status, you can choose between all open or overdue. I'll select "All" and then click "Apply" to generate a list of customers meeting the criteria, known as the recipients' list. If there is a customer you don't want to send statement to, simply uncheck the box next to their name.

When ready, you can print or preview the statements. Click on "Print or Preview" in the middle section. Each customer will have a separate statement displaying their activity from January 1 to January 31. The statement begins with the balance forward from the previous month. The total due is prominently displayed, and customers have a designated area to input the amount enclosed if paying by check. At the bottom, the statement breaks down the currently due amount, along with totals in various categories. This comprehensive overview helps customers understand their account status.

You can customize the date range and send statements to specific customers as needed. Once you have printed the statements, there's no need to save or send them within QuickBooks. Simply close the window using the X at the top, and they will be ready for printing at your convenience

The Tag Feature Of QuickBooks Online

The tags feature will allow you to create certain words that will appear on a drop-down when you are in different transactions in QuickBooks, and you can choose those. Later, you can use those to search for things or to run reports based on those tags.

If you are familiar with Gmail, we have got something similar in there where we can create a list and tag different emails and then search for anything that would have that particular tag we're looking for. This is still in beta right now.

Let me give you an example of how you might use this feature.

we have a feature in QuickBooks called classes, and we have kind of been using that in the way that tags will work. But let us say that you have an attorney's office, and you have four different attorneys in that office. You might want to run reports on the company as a whole, but you might also want to run reports on each attorney. If you had this list of classes set up, you could just pick from the drop-down list in each transaction you are in, which attorney that this should be tagged to. And we are going to use tags in the exact same way

The way you are going to access your tags option is through the gear icon on the top right-hand side of your screen, and underneath the list, right here as shown below;

You will now see the 'Tags' feature. Currently, we have not set up any tags yet, but once we create our first tag, you will notice the top of the tag screen changing with sections for 'Money In' and 'Money Out.' Let me illustrate with an example of how we will use tags.

Consider a company named Craig's Design and Landscape Services, which engages in both design work and pest control. Within their design work, they focus on three areas: fountains, landscaping, and sprinklers. We can organize tags into groups, and you will see the groups listed alongside the tags.

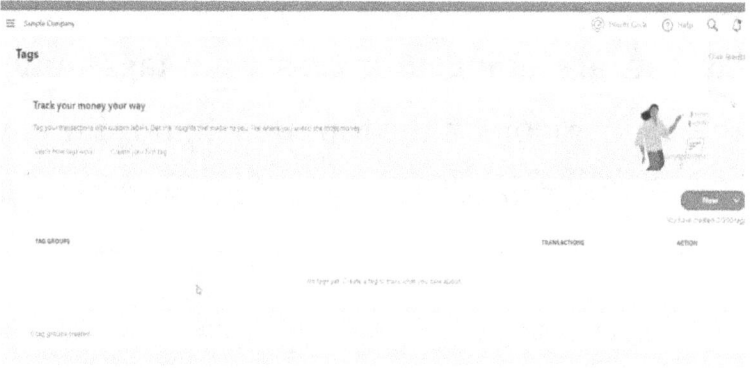

Let us start by creating a single tag.

Under 'New,' I will select 'Tag,' and let us use 'fountains' as our first tag.

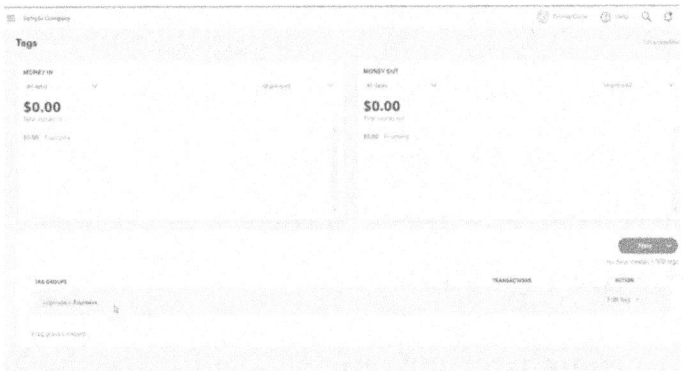

Create new tag   ×

Tag name

Group

If I wanted to place it in a group, I could, but as of now, I will hit 'Save' at the bottom. Now you will see the first tag named 'fountains,' currently ungrouped.

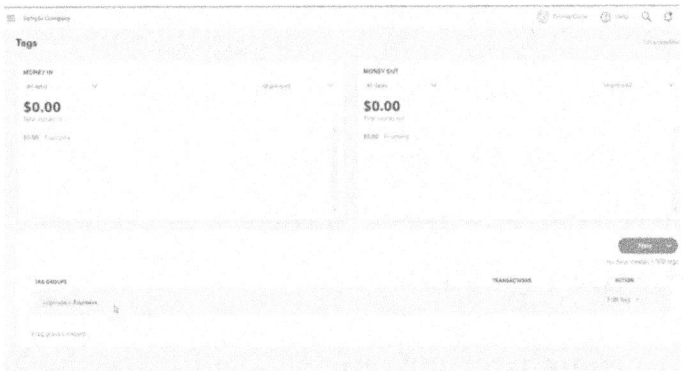

Regarding 'Money In' and 'Money Out,' once we apply these tags to transactions, we can analyze the financial impact based on these tags. Now, let's create a group to further illustrate.

I will create a tag group called 'design' and another one later called 'pest control.' To do this just click on new and select tag group.

Notice that I can add tags directly from this screen without going back to 'New Tag.' I will add two more tags: 'fans' and 'landscaping,' and also 'sprinklers.' Clicking 'Done' shows the 'design group', and clicking the drop-down arrow besides the group name "design" reveals the two tags within.

Now, 'fans' remains ungrouped. To add it to the 'design' group, I click 'Edit Tag,' select the 'design' group, and save it. Now 'design' displays three tags underneath.

Let's create one more tag group called 'pest control.' Under this group, I will add tags for 'residential' and 'commercial' customers. After adding them, I will click 'Done.'

At the bottom, you can see two tags: 'pest control' and 'design.' Additionally, notice the color blue. Each tag group can have a distinctive color scheme. I can change

174

the color by selecting 'Edit Group.' For example, I will choose yellow for this group. Saving it also applies the color to all tags within that group.

Now, let me show you where these tags and tag groups come into play—in any transaction. Suppose I create a new invoice.

Get back to your navigation pane and click new, the under customers as usual select invoice, on the invoice you will find an option labeled "tags."

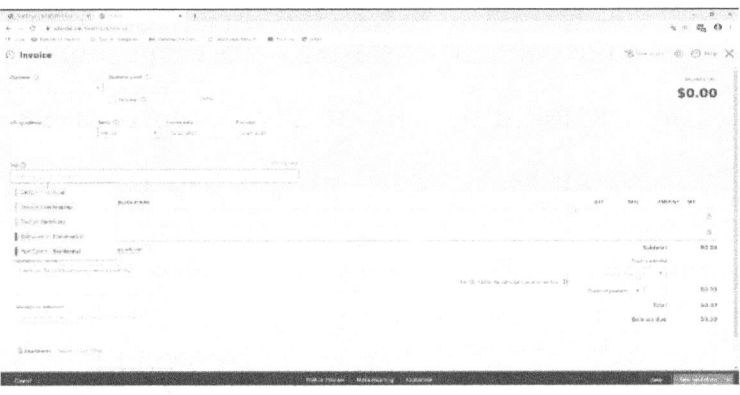

You can select from the drop-down list, and if needed, choose more than one. For example, you might tag items with labels like fountains or commercial. These tags will be useful for organizing and filtering information.

Now, let's set up an example:

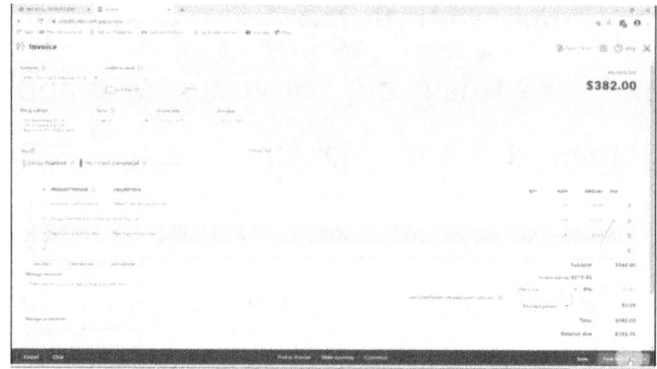

From above picture, we choose Tom Allen and select a product or service. Let's say it's priced at $50. For the next item, we pick fountains, specifically a rock fountain priced at $275. Additionally, we added pest control for this rock fountain to prevent bugs. After making these selections, clicking "Save and Close" will store the information.

Upon returning to the tags, we can assess the financial impact.

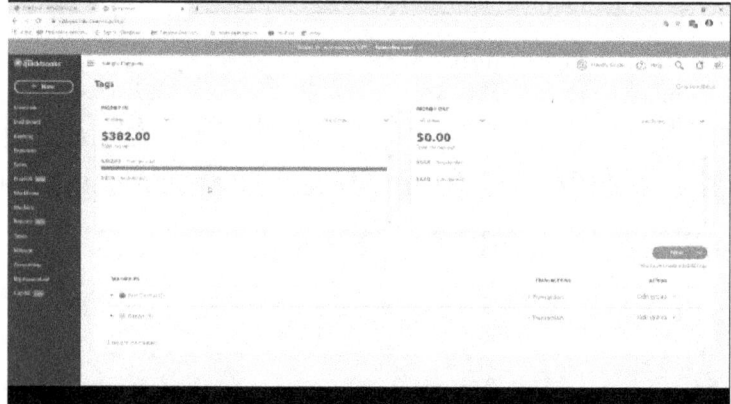

In this case, we see $382 under "money in." QuickBooks considers the moment an invoice is created as part of your income. Transactions like writing a check or using a credit card fall under "money outside." If, for instance, you bought materials related to one of these (money out) and tagged those transactions, you would see the money out reflected there. Tags offer a powerful feature to analyze where your money is coming in or going out.

Chapter Eight

Customer And Sales Reports

Having understood what tag is, let us now explore some reports related to customers and sales in QuickBooks. Navigating to the Reports section, we will focus on "Who owes you" and the categories underneath. A common report is the open invoices list, displaying customers who still owe money. Each transaction provides details like date and amount. You can click on a transaction to view and modify it, with changes reflected in the report upon saving.

Another valuable report is the customer balance detail under "Who owes you." This report presents all transactions for each customer, job, or sub-customer. To customize, select "Customize" in the top right, and under "Filter," choose "unpaid." Now, you can view each transaction associated with customers or jobs.

These reports offer insights into your financial interactions and are essential for regular assessments of your company's performance.

Let's dive back into reports for a moment. Going down to "Who owes you," there are other reports worth exploring. For instance, you might find a collections report valuable, offering comprehensive customer information, including phone numbers for potential follow-up calls.

Returning to reports, you will find options such as accounts receivable aging detail and aging summary. Summaries provide a total line item, while details break down every component of a category or line item. There's a variety of lists to explore, including invoices, terms, and statements under "Who owes you."

Moving on to sales and customer reports, you can generate a customer contact list, containing essential details like phone numbers and emails. Explore estimates by customer, track income by customer, and delve into payment methods, product lists, and services. Sales can be analyzed by customer, product, or even by time or activities.

Most reports are customizable. For example, with a sale by customer detail report, you can adjust the report period, group entries by customer or product, and explore different ways to organize the information. It's essential to note that reports are automatically set to accrual basis, reflecting income when invoiced, regardless of payment status. You can, however, adjust this basis per report. We will delve into this further when we explore profit and loss later.

This overview aims to showcase the available reports for customers and sales, primarily falling under these two categories (sales and customer).

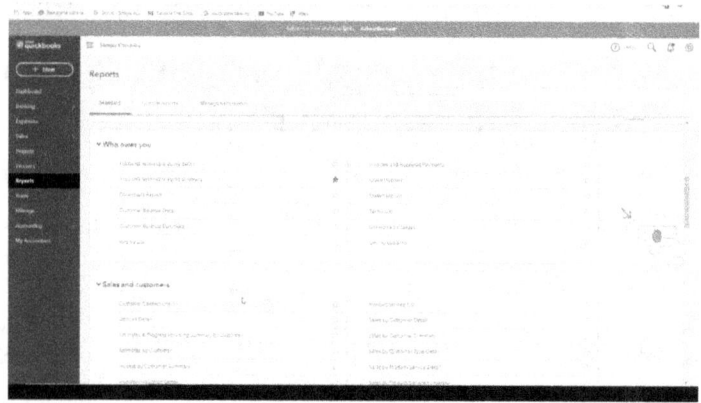

Overview Of Products And Services

Here, we will discuss how these elements function in QuickBooks. Products and services encompass items you either sell or purchase, and setting them up correctly is crucial for accurate inventory and profit/loss reports.

To access your products and services list, click on the gear icon at the top right of your screen and navigate to "Products and Services." This list includes everything you sell or buy which have set up, categorized by type. You will find service items you provide like landscaping and pest control, as well as physical inventory items. For instance, when looking at "rock fountain," you will observe the current stock and have the option to add more or sell existing items that you have. Diverse types of items populate this list, including non-inventory items. These are physical items present in the background, not tracked in terms of quantity but essential for buying or selling. As you peruse the list, you will observe item names, SKU numbers (if set up), item types, and descriptions that automatically appear when used on invoices or forms in QuickBooks. The sales price is visible, though it might vary for each customer, often set during invoicing or purchasing. Inventory items display quantity on hand and reorder points; however, this exercise lacks the setup for reorder points. The final column, the action column, provides options to edit items, make them inactive, or adjust quantities on hand. This is where your comprehensive list of products and services resides.

Adding New Products And Services

Now, let's move on to setting up these products and services. In this Section, I will guide you through the process. After the quick overview of the products and services screen, let's dive into creating your own. Whether your business has a handful or thousands, the process is the same.

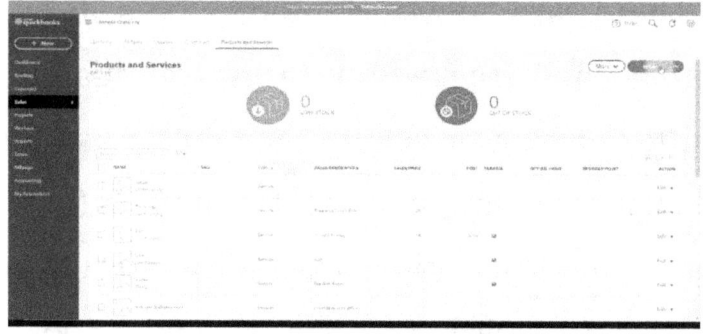

To add a new product or service, head to the "new" option in the products and services window. The first decision is to specify the type: inventory, non-inventory, or service. Inventory items are tracked, reminding you to reorder when supplies are low. Non-inventory items are physical, but you don't track quantities. Services, on the other hand, are intangible offerings. These three can also be bundled; for instance, a gift basket can include various items.

For this example, let's set up a service;

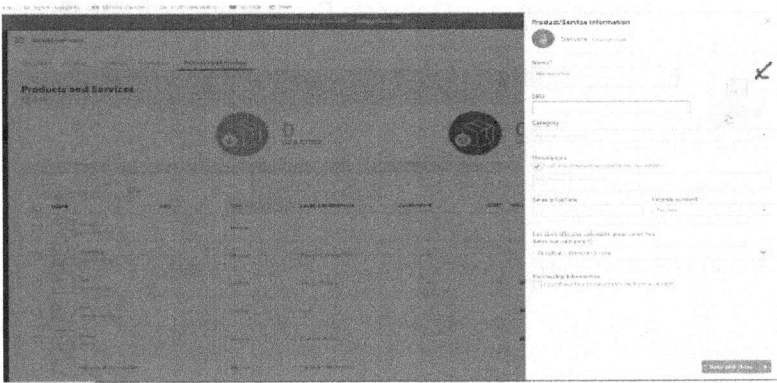

First, name your service; for instance, "maintenance." Optionally, input SKU numbers (if you have for your business) and attach a relevant picture of your product (where I indicated with blue arrow in the above picture). Categorize it under existing or new categories like design or landscaping. You can add new category by clicking under category and selecting the add new option from the drop-down options. Provide a clear description for invoices, such as "quarterly maintenance." If it has a fixed price, input it; otherwise, leave it blank. This overview will help you start creating your own products and services. Now, let's proceed to

Section Two for a hands-on demonstration on the product/sales information window.

On this screen, nothing transpires until you buy or sell the product or service; that's when the numbers come into play on your reports. Let's assume a flat rate of $250 per quarter for this example. The crucial element here is the income account selection when putting this on an invoice. The default is "services income," a suitable choice, but you have the flexibility to assign it to any income account of your preference.

Choosing an income account is paramount. If left unselected, QuickBooks won't prompt you, but your reports will be inaccurately skewed, leaving you perplexed. Focus on the word "income"; it explicitly indicates the necessity to direct the funds to an income account. If this pertains to a taxable product or service, you specify its taxability under "sales tax category): – taxable or non-taxable. Generally, services are non-taxable, while physical items are taxable.

Under preferred vendor is where fill vendor information if it happens to be a particular product or service that you buy from a vendor that you like, you can check the box and put in the vendor information but for this case I'm going to go ahead and uncheck the box for vendor and click Save and close at the bottom.

Back on the product and service window, you will notice that I have a new service in my list there called maintenance and you can see all of the information all the way across.

I can edit any of the information by clicking on edit there (under the action column that will take me back to this screen and I can change whatever I need to then save and close again. Then it will be updated.

You do have a couple of other actions you can take under this drop-down arrow under "Action" you can make this service inactive if you need to. You can also run a report on this service or you can duplicate it.

That is a quick way to go ahead and set up your new products and services.

Now that you know how to set up a service let's go ahead and look at setting up an inventory product; that way you can see how to tell QuickBooks how many you currently have on hand and then you can see how inventory is added to or deducted from that number.

Adding Inventory Product

On this section we will be dealing on how to add new products and services in QuickBooks, let us talk specifically about adding inventory products. True inventory means that you want to keep a count on how many of these products you have in your office, you want QuickBooks to let you know when you get low so that you can order some more. You will want to actually know how many you have on hand when you first set up your new inventory product and once you have done that, then as you invoice customers that is how your products will get out of inventory and as you purchase them that is how your products will get back into inventory.

Flip over to QuickBooks with me and I will show you how to add an inventory product. You are going to add an inventory product the same way we added the new products and services earlier. Get to the top of your products and services list; choose the new option.

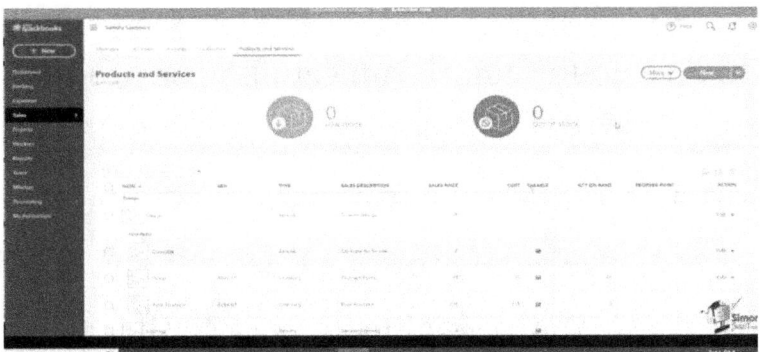

This time we are going to choose inventory.

The first thing you are going to do is give your inventory a name. I'm going to call mine sprinkler clamps and then we are going to give it a SKU; I will call this one 55 and then we will choose a category and let's say in this case that we are going to put it under landscaping. Next, you fill initial quantity on hand; this means you are going to do a count before you set up your product and if you have 10 in the back room, you are going to put that in there and that gives it a starting number. You also want to have a date to start this with and let's just say in this case, that I want to go back to the beginning of February. On reorder point; what this means is what number do you want to get down to before QuickBooks pops up and tells you that you need to order some more. So, input whatever number you want there. Let us just say in this case when we get down two three the next thing you are going to see is inventory asset account (do not change this); this is the account that the value of the inventory will actually go into in your chart of accounts. Remember that inventory is an asset to your business, you are worth more because you have it right now but your goal is to sell it and get it out the door. So that is the asset account the inventory will sit in and then we're going to put in a description. I would put in the same thing "sprinkler clamps" and then if you have a set rate than you charge for the inventory, you will want to type this in but if you don't have one (that's different every single time) then, you can just leave a blank. let's say that we sell it for two dollars and seventy-five cents. Next is the income account which you don't want to change either because this is the income account that your inventory will go into when you make a sale. When I put sprinkler clamps on an invoice and I sell this it will go into that sales product income account. If the inventory is a taxable product, you will select taxable under the "sales tax category".

Next, we have the purchasing information; this was the selling information up there. This is when you purchase it, down here the first thing it asks for is a description. When you order this particular inventory product from whatever company you order them from, what is their description. Sometimes it will be the same and other times it might have a part number. At the end there is just all kinds of different things that this could say. Below this purchasing information is the "cost"; this means on average what do you buy it for. It does not mean that the last time you purchase this it was a dollar seventy-five. let's just say on average though it is a dollar seventy-five and it will go to an expense account called cost of goods sold. If you have a preferred vendor then you can pick them from the list there on "preferred vendor" tab. It could be that you like to get these from Hicks hardware and that's all you need to tell it. Then click Save and close at the bottom.

At this point, I should see my sprinkler clamps right there, you can see the SKU number we typed in the sale price, the cost, under quantity on hand there's ten currently and when it gets down to three it is going to pop up and ask us if you want to order some more. Don't forget you have some options over there under your action column. If you wanted to go into just the quantity maybe you discovered there is really only 9 in the back room, you will be able to do that. You also have the ability to adjust the starting value and that is really all there is to adding inventory products

Purchase Orders

If your company buys a lot of products you might want to create a purchase order system for your business when you do this, it's a way of actually tracking everything you have ordered and that way you can see what has come in. If there's anything back ordered that sort of thing and this is also going to be a way to start the process of receiving your items into inventory. let me go ahead and show you how to create a purchase order but before we get started, there is a couple things that you need to know first of all. If you would like to use the purchase order feature in QuickBooks, you have to be enrolled in the QuickBooks Online Plus edition; that is the Edition that actually handles purchase orders. The other thing is you are going to have to actually turn on the purchase order feature in the account settings.

So, to do that, go up to the gear icon; you are going over to accountant settings make sure you click on expenses and there is where you see purchase orders.

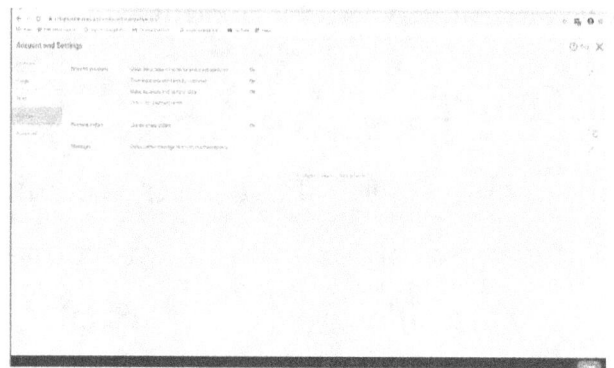

If this is not on, just come over to the pencil icon and then make sure you check the box for the purchase order. Once that is done, you are good to use the purchase order features. Then go ahead and close with the X.

Now let's go and look really quick at our products and services so we discuss how we going to order some more and put it into our inventory. Click on the gear icon under the list the second column, click on products and services. If you remember, we talked about some of these things we had set under our product and services being inventory and one of them that I want to talk about right here is going to be the "Rock fountain"

Now let's say we have two of it but we are getting ready to do a new job and we need to order two more to have a total of four.

To create a new purchase, go to the navigation bar and click on new and down on the second column click on purchase order.

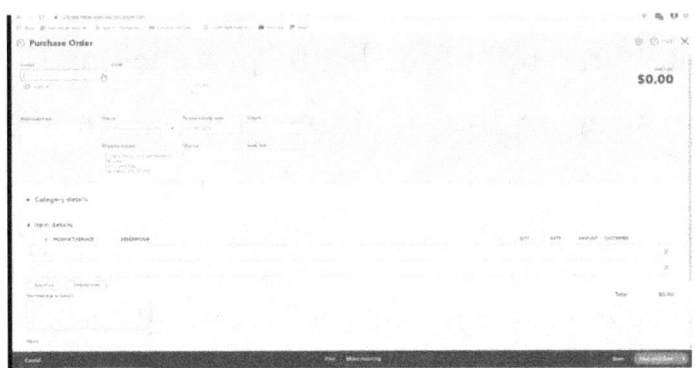

The first thing I need to do when creating a purchase order is to pick my vendor. I'm going to go down the list there and pick Hicks hardware. If I had Hicks hardware's email it would be pulled in right there on the email tab. let's talk about the ship – for a second. If you want to have Hicks Hardware ship these directly to your customer, you can choose your customer under "ship to" if not, then it is just going to come to your office. You do not need to choose anything there. You fill your date of purchase under "purchase order date" and in this case they are using the crew number field so we are going to plug something in there. You can also set a "ship via" which would say USPS FedEx. You can also set a sales rep if you had those as well. Scroll down the list, you use the "item details" not the "category details" and remember we are getting ready to order some more rock fountains. Now let's take the existing ones except "rock fountains" out of the list by just clicking the little trash can over on the right and put the number you want to order which in this case, I want to get two of it so that I have a total of four. If the order is related to a particular customer, you will plug that information in right under the customer column. If you were ordering other things as well you can go ahead and fill it as you did with" rock fountains". You have a place to put a message to your vendor, a memo and at the bottom some attachments. Once this is done, you will send this over to your vendor. Then click save and close.

And that is how that works. If you have the vendors email address you could have emailed this directly to them other than that maybe, you called them on the phone and ordered it but you do have your Pio in there; so that whenever you go to receive these items, you have something to receive it against. That is how you actually create a purchase order.

The next step in the process is that your products actually come in and you are going to go in and receive those products into your inventory.

Receiving products into inventory

Now that you have created a purchase order, you can actually receive the items into your inventory. The logical process is that once you order the items from your vendor, they are going to come in the next week (10 days probably) and you are going to want to receive them into your inventory.

Head over to QuickBooks so I guide you through the process.

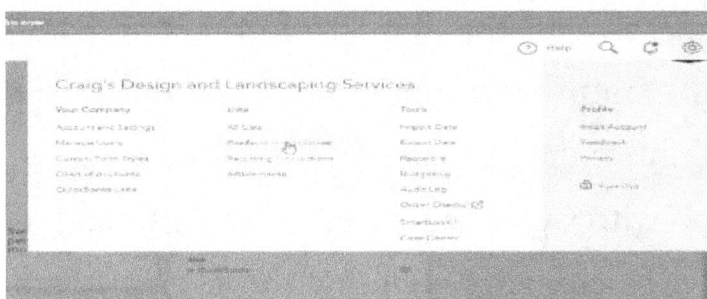

Click on the gear icon and under list column, select product and services. If we go down and look at rock film, we still just have two and that is because all we have done at this point is order two more. Once we get through this receiving product into inventory feature, then you are going to notice that the number will go up to four. All you have to do is head over to the navigation bar and click on new and create a new bill. The first thing it asks you is who is your vendor and this is where I'm going to pick Hicks Hardware. Once vendor name is submitted, a little window will pop up on the right and this is letting me know that I have an open purchase order.

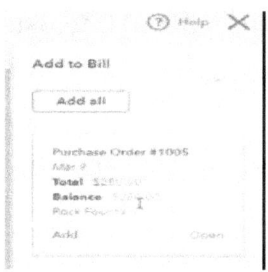

To seamlessly add the items from this purchase order to the bill, simply click on it (Add). As you scroll down, you will notice the inclusion of the rock fountains – two of them, with specified rates, amounts, and all the details we discussed. Given that this is an authentic bill from the vendor, precision in verifying their rates and amounts is crucial. If a sale occurred (explaining the order of two), we would adjust the rate accordingly, resulting in a corresponding change in the amount.

Returning to the top, you will see that our mailing address for Hicks Hardware has been automatically populated. We need to select the terms specified in the bill – let's go with Net 30. Specify the bill date, denoting when it was printed, and the due date, indicating when it is payable. Enter the bill number on the designated space, and that essentially covers our necessary tasks. There's a memo section at the bottom left, and we can attach files if needed. Once satisfied, click 'save and close.'

Now, we go back and check the current inventory (on your product and services window). For rock fountains, we now have four in stock. This illustrates one avenue through which items enter inventory – via a purchase order. Later, we'll explore alternative methods like writing checks or using debit cards. However, this method focuses on creating an order and efficiently processing its reception

Product And Services Report

Certainly! Here, I'd like to explore some reports related to products and services. In this final section, let's delve into specific reports associated with products and services. The repository boasts numerous reports, and I encourage you to revisit those we have not discussed to grasp the full spectrum of available options.

Now, let's transition to QuickBooks, where I'll guide you through accessing these product and service reports.

Navigate to your handy navigation pane and click on "reports."

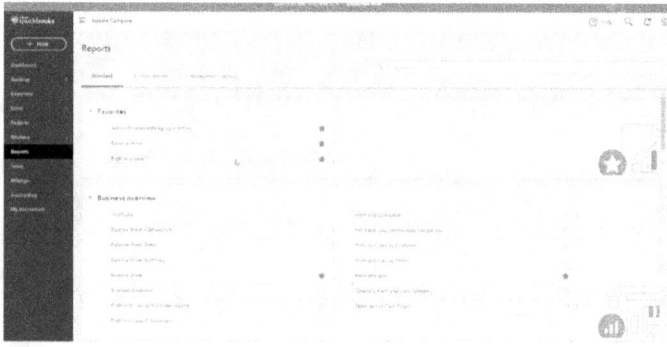

If you have earmarked some reports as favorites, they will appear at the top as favorites. Otherwise, let's scroll down until you encounter the section labeled "expenses and vendors. "Within this section, you will find your purchase order reports. There are two types: one is a list, and the other is the purchase order detail. Let's commence with the list. Here, you will find all open purchase orders neatly organized by vendor. It is worth noting that once you have received your items from a purchase order, it's no longer considered open and won't be listed here.

Explore the options at the top. Currently, we are displaying purchase orders for all dates, and they are conveniently grouped by vendor. For more customization, you can refine the filter options. Choose specific vendors from the list, or opt to see all vendors. I'll go ahead and run the report, yielding the same results as I focused on open purchase orders.

Now, let's return to the reports list and delve into what we term the "open purchase order detail." Adjusting the dates, you may notice an empty report reflecting only March first. However, selecting "all dates" and running the report reveals a comprehensive view. Now, I have a clear view of the purchase orders and their detailed information. This means that every line item in the purchase order is displayed. Currently, I'm grouping them by product or service. I might switch to grouping them by vendor and run that report – and, of course, there is only one vendor in this instance. Additionally, I have the same customized options I demonstrated just a minute ago. If you wish to choose filter options, you have that flexibility. If you want like to modify the header and footer options, located in this area up here, you can make those edits and then run the report once your changes are made.

Now, let us return to the report list. I want like to mention some other reports here that do not specifically pertain to purchase orders, but you will find them useful. If you want to examine purchases by vendor, that is an option. You might also explore purchases by product or delve into a transaction list by vendor, or check out the vendor contact list – you can see those reports there. With numerous reports available, it is advisable to run them regularly to stay informed about what is happening and ensure accurate data in QuickBooks.

Using Payroll On QuickBooks Online

Before you can run payroll in QuickBooks Online payroll, you need to add your employees. Let's go over how to add your employees, including their personal info pay rates, pay schedules, work location, and deductions. We'll also show you how to make this easier by inviting your employees to add some of this info themselves.

To start, go to payroll.

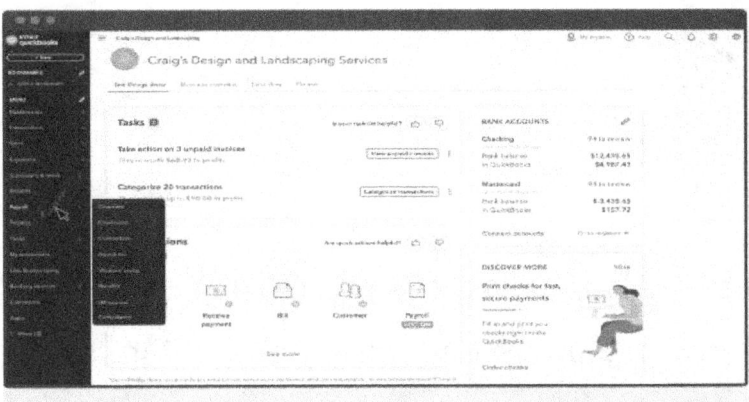

If you're setting up, select start under "Tell us about your team";

If you've been running payroll already, select employees;

If you're setting up payroll for the first time, you will be asked how you have run your payroll before switching to QuickBooks;

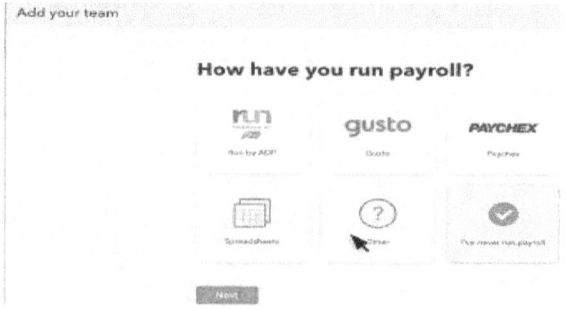

You may be able to upload employee reports from your prior payroll service and then have QuickBooks import some of your employee details for you. But to do it yourself directly on QuickBooks click next and Select "Add Employee".

Add your employees name and email address and hire date.

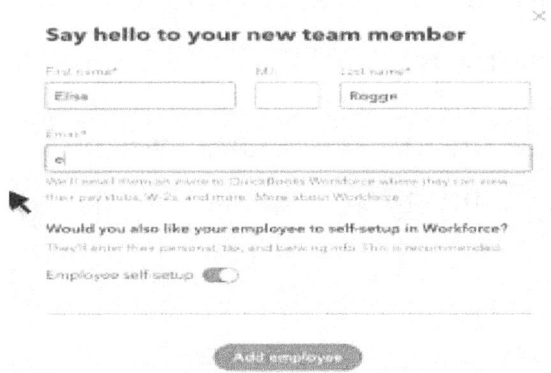

QuickBooks will automatically email them an invite to QuickBooks workforce where they can view their paystubs, W-2s and more. To save you some data entry. You can have your employees enter their personal tax withholding and bank account info themselves. Select add employee.

Now you are ready to add your employee info You can start with any section;

Since employee's self-setup is on. You won't be able to edit some fields in the personal info tax withholding or payment method cards.

When you Click on edit at left hand side on the personal inform tab, it will take you to the window pane below where you can view or set up the employee's info;

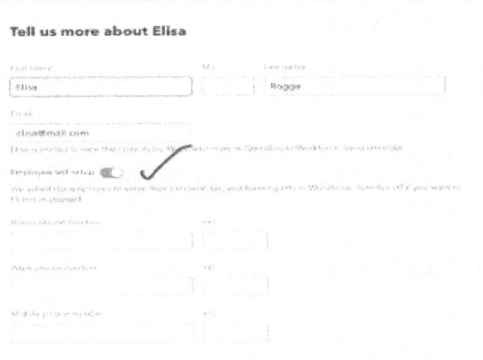

If you need to pay your employees right away or want to add the info yourself, turn off employee self-setup (where I mark blue in the above picture). You can turn it on or off at any time and once turned off, it will pop up a message window as shown below;

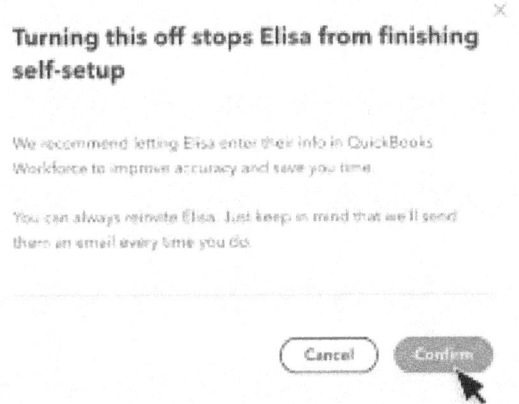

You can either click confirm or cancel. If I click confirm, it will take back to the personal info window. If I decide to turn on the employee self-set up again, it will still pop up a message window as below;

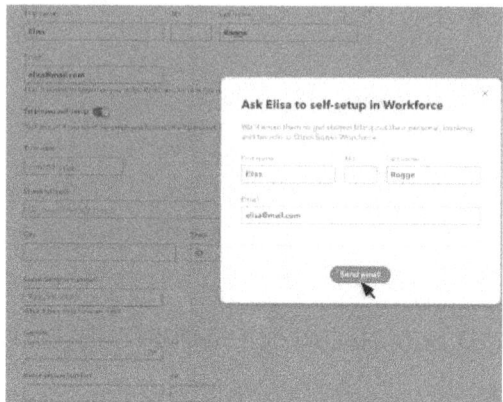

Then you will click the send mail and save.

Once your employee adds their info through QuickBooks workforce, you will be able to see it and make changes.

Scroll down and let's start with employment details;

Select start;

Add your employees, hire date pace, schedule and work location. All of the other fields are optional.

For a pay schedule, click on the pencil icon and;

Tell us how often you pay this employee, when their next pay day will be and when the last day of that pay period will be. The pay day is the day your employees get their checks or direct deposits. But the pay period is the days you are paying your employee for. QuickBooks payroll shows you the next four pay days and pay periods based on the info you entered. So, you can check that everything is correct. You can name this schedule and if you want to use it for other employees, just check the box at the bottom. If everything looks good. Select Save.

Next, you will need to add a work location;

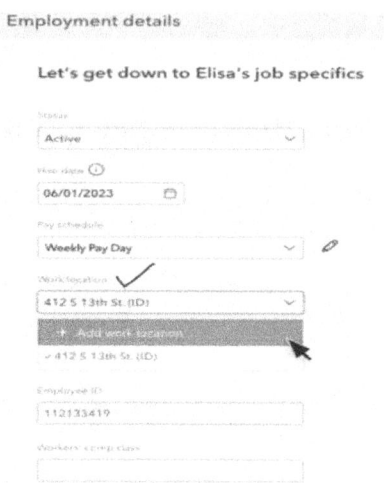

The work location is the physical address where your employee works. You'll see the address you gave us when you added your business details. If your employee is based out of a different location, add a new location when you're finished. Select save.

For pay types, tell us how much you pay your employee. You can choose from hourly, salary, or commission only. For this example, we'll set up an hourly rate. As you scroll down the window, you can also add other pay types like overtime or bonus, and you can set up time off policies.

Select additional pay types for other items like reimbursement or tips when you are done. Select Save.

If your employee has deductions like 401k, health insurance, or garnishments like child support, or if your business contributes to employee's retirement or health insurance, add them by selecting start on deductions and contribution.

Select add deduction contribution or add garnishment. Then fill out the details and select save When finished adding all the deductions, select done. You've added your new team member. Nice work.

Repeat these steps for all employees.

How To Erase Your QuickBooks Online Data And Start Over

You can erase all your QuickBooks Online company data and start over again if you need to. How just depends on how long you've had your subscription. If you've had your subscription for more than 60 days then cancel your subscription.

Select Settings (by clicking on the gear icon), under your company select Account and settings and then the Billing and Subscription tab.

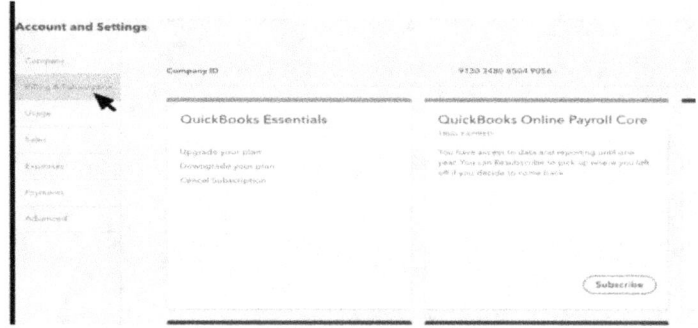

In the QuickBooks Online box select cancel subscription. That's it. Just sign up for a new account and start over.

QuickBooks will hold onto your old data for up to a year. If your subscription is less than 60 days, then edit the url and replace "homepage"

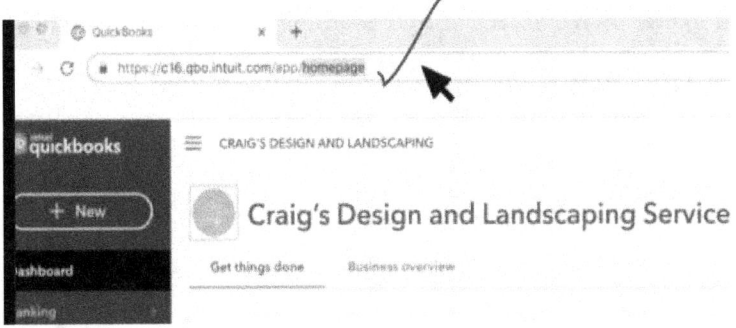

"with "purge company" and hit enter.

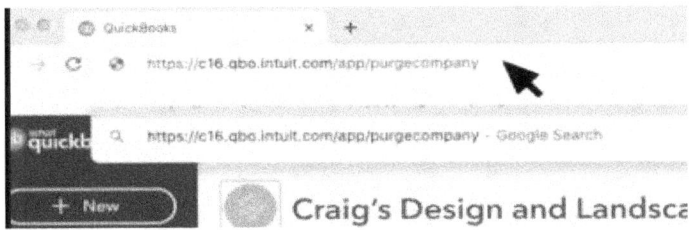

This will delete all your company data so make sure that's what you want to do. Once you are ready, type Yes in the box and select OK.

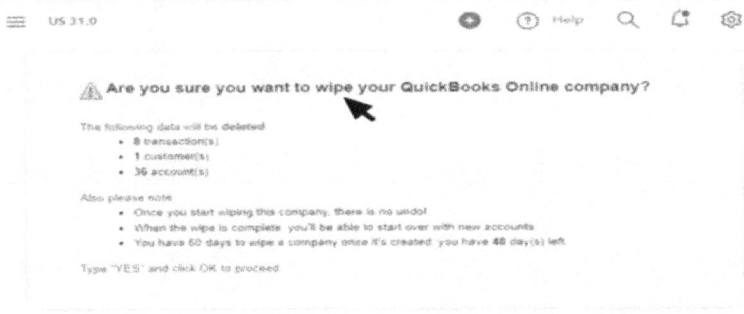

You will get a confirmation message from QuickBooks and then you can start entering in your new company data. If you run into issues doing this, try the steps again in Incognito mode.

www.ingramcontent.com/pod-product-compliance
Lightning Source LLC
Chambersburg PA
CBHW071039290526

45795CB00004B/1218